JOBS AND EARNINGS FOR STATE CITIZENS:
Monitoring the Outcomes of State Economic Development and Employment and Training Programs

RICHARD E. WINNIE
HARRY P. HATRY
VIRGINIA B. WRIGHT

September 1977

5039-3

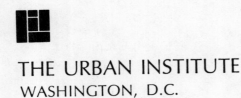

THE URBAN INSTITUTE
WASHINGTON, D.C.

        This work has been supported by the U.S. Economic Development Administra-
tion, the National Center for Productivity and the Quality of Working Life,
and the states of North Carolina and Wisconsin. The states of North Carolina
and Wisconsin have also participated in various portions of this work.

        The interpretations and conclusions are those of the authors and are
not necessarily those of The Urban Institute, its trustees, or organizations
that support its research.

ISBN 87766-208-8

UI 5039-3

PLEASE REFER TO URI 19900 WHEN ORDERING

Available from:

Publications Office
The Urban Institute
2100 M Street, N.W.
Washington, D.C. 20037

List price: $4.00

A/77/3M

PREFACE

This report on procedures for monitoring the outcome of state economic development services is one of a series of reports on ways to measure the outcomes of basic state government services. Other reports deal with transportation, social services, mental health, chronic disease control programs, and corrections.

Concerned citizens and government officials--in particular, service agency personnel, budget and planning staffs, legislators, and gubernatorial staffs--have become increasingly concerned about the effectiveness of government services. Little useful information is currently regularly available on the effectiveness of such services in meeting the needs of their clientele. The research leading to this series of reports was, therefore, undertaken as an initial step toward developing procedures that would enable jurisdictions to obtain such information. Though the work was directed toward state governments, much of the material also seems to be applicable to regional and local agencies.

This series of reports is an initial effort in what is a very large task. Several of the procedures outlined in the reports need considerable development--steps that may require the investment of significant financial and staff resources. Despite its exploratory character, the work completed indicates that considerably improved effectiveness information can be made available on a regular basis.

This report focuses on the outcomes (or end results) of services that agencies concerned with economic development should monitor and on the procedures for regularly collecting data on these outcomes. Such data, collected over a period of time, can indicate trends, progress, and problems. Consequently, outcome information can be an important aid to public officials and concerned citizens in determining what is being accomplished and for identifying areas that need examination. These procedures are, however, no substitute for program evaluation methods (such as "controlled" experiments and sophisticated techniques of statistical analysis) that attempt to identify specific effects of specific programs.

The research that led to these reports was carried out by The Urban Institute and the states of North Carolina and Wisconsin, with the cooperation of the National Association of State Budget Officers. The primary sources of support for this volume were the Economic Development Administration and the National Center for Productivity and Quality of Working Life. The U.S. Department of Health, Education, and Welfare, the U.S. Department of Transportation, and the Ford Foundation also provided financial support for these efforts.

The authors hope that these reports will increase awareness of the information needed to reflect citizen and client concerns regarding public services, encourage state and local governments to consider, develop, and use these or similar measurement procedures, and stimulate further research and developmental efforts to produce reliable outcome measurement techniques.

CONTENTS

APPENDIX

ACKNOWLEDGMENTS

This report is based upon a project sponsored by the National Center for Productivity and the Quality of Working Life, the National Association of State Budget Officers, The Urban Institute, the state governments of North Carolina and Wisconsin, and the Economic Development Administration of the U.S. Department of Commerce.

The project team in North Carolina was coordinated by Kenneth Howard, Budget Director, and Gloria Grizzle, Ann Janzen, and Gayle Burleson of the state budget office. Also participating on the North Carolina project team were Susan Adams, Tony Baker, Ronald Bloom, Robert Fitzgerald, Al Haskins, Larry Hodes, John Morris, Robert Weiss, and Gil Wilson of the Department of Administration. Important assistance was also contributed by Kenneth Daly, Connie Janssen, and Fanny Chestnut-Andrews of the office of Employment and Training and Larry McGee and Michael Rakouskas of the Department of Natural and Economic Resources.

In Wisconsin the project was coordinated by Bernard Mrazik of the Department of Administration. Also participating were Charles Hedrick of the Planning Office, Richard Seaman and Ray Mueller of the Business Development Department, and Harvey Sokolow, Kathy McElroy, Ronald Geason, and Cilla Reesman of the staff of the State Manpower Council.

Donald M. Fisk of The Urban Institute developed many of the initial measurement concepts.

The following provided helpful reviews of drafts of this report: George Bell and J. Donald Judy, National Association of State Budget Officers; Seymour Brandwein, Director of the Office of Program Planning and Evaluation of the U.S. Department of Labor; Douglas Frechtling and Steven Muha, U.S. Travel Data Center; Jack Cawthorne, National Association of State Development Agencies; Robert Wise and David Hartley, Conference of State Planning Agencies; and Charles Holt and Carl Snead of The Urban Institute.

SUMMARY

This report discusses procedures that can be used by state governments to monitor programs aimed at improving employment and earnings of state citizens. These include programs designed to stimulate new employment opportunities and increase the earnings of state citizens by industrial development and tourism promotion and to improve the well-being of individual citizens through employment and training activities.

The measurement procedures presented in this report are designed to indicate changes in the economic condition and economic status of individuals and households affected by economic development programs. The measures are intended for use by governors' offices, state budget and planning staffs, state legislatures, and state economic development agencies. The data collection procedures described herein are designed to be of relatively low cost and within the technical capabilities of state governments, in order to enable states to obtain this information annually.

The overall purposes of state economic development activities are to improve the availability, duration, and quality of individual employment, increase employee income, avoid detrimental impacts on the environment and energy reserves, and increase or at least maintain citizen satisfaction with their standard of living. A set of measures and data collection procedures for these objectives are presented in Chapter 1.

Industrial development and tourism promotion are two major economic development strategies used by state governments. Industrial development activities aim at attracting new firms to the state and encouraging expansion, or at least continuation of firms already in the state. Tourism promotion uses advertising and other promotional services to attract tourists. Both these programs seek to increase the number of employment opportunities and the amount of earnings of state citizens. Chapters 2 and 3 identify outcome measures and data collection procedures for industrial development and tourism promotion, respectively.

Employment and training programs assist economic development by providing services directly to individuals. They seek to help the unemployed obtain jobs and to improve the duration of employment, income and quality of the job of individuals. Chapter 4 presents outcome measures and data collection procedures for these programs.

While state economic development programs are intended to benefit the state as a whole, they often are aimed at upgrading specific "underdeveloped" regions or population groups that are less well off than other residents. Target populations vary among states and types of programs but can be generally defined by geographic region, demographic characteristics, or income levels.

This report emphasizes the need for monitoring the economic status of both the state as a whole and substate regions and population subgroups, and suggests methods of obtaining data for these purposes.

This report is the result of a one-year research effort conducted in cooperation with the planning and budget offices, economic development agencies, and employment and training agencies of North Carolina and Wisconsin. The first step was to identify measures now being used to monitor or evaluate state or regional economic development. This was done through reviews of the budget documents of all state governments and special studies made in some states, through discussions with officials of national organizations and federal agencies concerned with industrial development, travel promotion, or employment and training, and through ongoing dialogues with employees of the North Carolina and Wisconsin state governments. Based on this work, a set of measures and corresponding data collection procedures were developed. Both the measures and data collection procedures were redrafted continually during the project to adapt them to considerations of feasibility and relevant available data. Little testing of measures and data collection procedures was possible during the short term of the project. The statewide employment and income survey described in Chapter 1 was the most important procedure tested-- both in North Carolina and Wisconsin.

The periodic measurement of outcomes recommended in this report will not provide information as to what degree specific government programs are causing the measured changes. Considerably more detailed analysis and, in many cases, sophisticated experiments would be necessary for such determinations.

Principal Measurement Approaches

The principal measurement approaches recommended are as follows.

Overall Measures of Economic Development (Chapter 1)

Data on the following are recommended to measure changes in conditions related to overall state economic development:

(a) Unemployment rates at specific points in time;

(b) Extent of unemployment of individuals and households during a specific period, such as twelve months (for example: the percentage of households in the state which experienced at least four weeks during the past twelve months when there was no member employed but at least one member sought work);

(c) Per capita income;

(d) The percentage and number of households with incomes less than that required for basic support;

(e) Environmental impact of firms located in the state, such as on achievement of air and water quality standards and energy conservation goals; and

(f) Citizens' satisfaction with their present standard of living.

To measure (a) and (c), states can use existing data developed by state bureaus of employment security, the Census Bureau, and the U.S. Bureau of Economic Analysis (BEA).

States presently lack annual data on (b), (d), and (f). An annual statewide survey of a sample of households is recommended to correct these deficiencies. In addition to providing this information, such a survey would permit its disaggregation by substate region and population subgroups and provide information on "discouraged workers" and "dissatisfied part-time employed." Considering the small sample size which would ordinarily be practical for states, however, only large subgroups could be used.

Appendix A contains an illustrative questionnaire for use in such a state-wide survey. Questions similar to these were included in recent test surveys conducted in Wisconsin and North Carolina. Based on those surveys, we estimate that a survey of 1,500 to 2,000 households would cost $25,000 to $40,000. If other state agencies (such as the transportation, health, and social service departments) cooperated in sponsoring such a survey to obtain information of interest to them as well, the cost to any one agency would be reduced.

A partial alternative to a state-sponsored survey that may become available in the future is for a state government to request that the Census Bureau provide weighted data tabulations from the annual March Current Population Survey (CPS) for the state and substate populations. This could provide data on duration of unemployment (b) and on annual income (d), but in both cases only for individuals and not for households. If the data can be obtained at low cost and sufficiently quickly, this could become a useful source of data.

It was not possible for this project to assess the adequacy of data on progress toward environmental and energy goals (e). It does appear that state agencies collect a great deal of data on environmental impact but very little in the energy area. Whether or not this data is suitable for this annual outcome monitoring purpose is as yet unstudied.

Industrial Development (Chapter 2)

Recommended measures of the outcome of state industrial development efforts include:

(a) The number of new or expanded firms that had contact with state industrial development agencies and the employment and payrolls of such firms;

(b) The number of jobs lost due to plant closures or major work force reductions;

(c) The number of former industrial prospects which indicate that their decision to locate in the state was significantly influenced by state actions—and the estimated number of new jobs and wages and salaries for them;

(d) The number of former industrial prospects which indicate that factors the state government could influence affected their decision not to locate in the state;

(e) Ratings by former industrial prospects of the quality of state assistance which they received; and

(f) Environmental impact of new or expanded firms, such as on air and water quality and energy conservation.

Most states estimate the number of jobs and payroll of a new or expanded firm shortly after a firm announces its decision to locate or expand in the state. These estimates often differ greatly from the number of jobs and payroll actually created because by the time a firm begins it may decide to reduce or increase the scale of its operations, or it may eliminate the project entirely. Therefore, it is recommended that outcome measures be based on actual employment and payroll data after the new operations begin, even though this will delay the availability of the data.

The major new procedure required by the items listed above is follow-up interviews with former industrial prospects. Appendix B contains an illustrative list of questions for use in such interviews. Follow-up contacts with firms that located in the state would provide employment and payroll data and a rough estimate of the significance of the assistance provided by the state. Contacts with firms which decided not to locate in the state would also obtain estimates of the importance of factors which affected the firms' decisions negatively.

Data on the number of new and expanded firms, and on the number of new jobs and the amount of new payrolls, should be tabulated for substate regions as well as for the state as a whole. These data should also be tabulated to reflect how new firms are contributing to the achievement of state objectives to stimulate employment and earnings of particular regions, to attract certain types of firms to reduce seasonal fluctuations, and to reduce detrimental environmental impacts.

Tourism Promotion (Chapter 3)

The recommended outcome measures for tourism promotion include:

(a) The number of tourism-related jobs;

(b) The dollar amount of tourist expenditures;

(c) The number of tourists from targeted areas who visited the state;

(d) The number of participants in state-sponsored promotional events and travel opportunities:

(e) The number and percent of households that visited the state after utilizing state-sponsored travel information services; and

(f) Ratings of the quality of state travel information services by households that utilized such services.

Most states make annual estimates of the impact of travel industries on state employment and income. These estimates often encompass types of travel, such as business travel, which are not a target of many state tourism promotion programs. Estimates of the impacts of tourism should include only those types of travel that are within the scope of a tourism promotion program.

In addition to measuring the impact of the overall program on employment and income, states should attempt to monitor the effects of particular components. For example, states often design promotional programs to attract particular types of travelers, such as conventioneers, persons interested in outdoor recreation, visitors to specific sites, and "pass-through" travelers. To measure the outcome of such specific promotional efforts, states should focus on year-to-year changes in employment and income in businesses most directly affected by each type of promotional activity. For example, changes in annual expenditures by users of campgrounds and associated services will help indicate whether state efforts to attract persons interested in outdoor recreation are effective.

Data for some of the suggested outcome measures (such as (e) and (b) above) can be obtained from a survey of households that used state-sponsored tourism information services (such as travel brochures, roadside information centers, and convention assistance). Appendix C contains an illustrative questionnaire for use in such a survey. The survey would obtain information on:

(a) Satisfaction of users with the relevance, timeliness, and overall helpfulness of the services;

(b) Whether users of the services visited or lengthened a visit to the state after they received services; and

(c) The users' perceptions of the extent to which the services may have been responsible for a positive decision.

Employment and Training Programs (Chapter 4)

We recommend that data be obtained on the following key aspects of employment and training programs:

(a) Postprogram employment and earnings records of former participants;

(b) Former participants' perceptions of program quality and value;

(c) Former participants' satisfaction with postprogram jobs (if employed); and

(d) Unmet need for employment and training services.

These data are not presently gathered regularly by state governments. A survey of at least a sample of former participants conducted about six months or one year after they have left the program seems appropriate. The data obtained would include information on employment and earnings, participants' perceptions of the quality and value of their training, and their satisfaction with postprogram jobs.

Chapter 4 (and Appendix D) provides an illustrative survey questionnaire and discussion of procedures. North Carolina conducted limited testing of some parts of this instrument in 1976; there also have been other ad hoc efforts at similar follow-up surveys.

In most cases it will be more feasible to attempt to contact a sample rather than all former participants. Telephone interviews are likely to be the most economical method of interview. Even then, surveys may cost as much as $10 to $15 or more per contact, since locating former participants can be a major problem.

A possible alternative to such a survey is to obtain information on former participants from government records, such as state unemployment compensation files or Social Security Administration (SSA) records. These records can be used either as the primary source of data for regular monitoring or for periodically validating data gathered by surveys of former participants. Such records, however, have important limitations. The data in them useful for monitoring are earnings by three-month (quarterly) periods. Since they do not include all workers, they cannot be used to monitor programs whose graduates tend to enter noncovered employment, such as government and certain agricultural occupations; however, this problem will be moderated considerably in the case of unemployment compensation records when unemployment insurance coverage is expanded in 1978 to cover approximately 97 percent of the labor force. In addition, special arrangements are needed to utilize the records for these purposes and to maintain data in government files beyond the period of routine destruction. Also, the three-month time periods for which earnings are reported will not always coincide well with the postprogram period being examined.

North Carolina conducted a feasibility study of using unemployment compensation records. The results indicated that postprogram employment in noncovered occupations was a major impediment to their use. The usefulness of these records may increase, however, due to the planned expansion in social security and unemployment compensation coverage.

Two major factors should be explicitly considered in analyses of postprogram earnings and employment: "case difficulty" and "external or nonprogram influences."

Case difficulty is the recognition that incoming clients differ in ability to achieve a positive postprogram result. Postprogram success is influenced by such client characteristics at intake as education, age, and previous work experience and earnings. To account for these differences, it is suggested that outcome data be grouped into three to five categories of case difficulty, based on characteristics which appear to be related to potential postprogram success.

"External influences," such as the level of unemployment in the county or region where the client resides, can also affect program success. The effects of external influences on postprogram results can be analyzed in part by classifying outcome data into three to five categories according to the level of unemployment or job vacancy rates in the region.

Participants' perceptions of the helpfulness of the services they received are gaining acceptance as a basis for monitoring employment and training programs. Factors which probably should be considered include: the clearness of instructions, the courtesy and helpfulness of staff, and the convenience of services. Participants' views should also be obtained on the extent to which the program actually had helped them obtain and perform postprogram jobs. A questionnaire designed to obtain this information might be administered either at program exit, if a suitable opportunity exists, or as part of the follow-up interview suggested above. The perceptions of both graduates and those who did not complete the program should be gathered. An illustrative list of questions is included in Appendix D.

An option is to compare the data on postprogram employment (such as number of weeks of employment and earnings) to the same data for similar length periods (such as six months or one year) before clients' entry into programs. This has many interpretation problems since the period prior to entry is likely to be an unusual one for many clients. If the period considered is less than one year, there may also be differences due to seasonal employment factors. In some cases, postprogram employment, even though not up to the level of preprogram employment, may nevertheless represent a real success for the program (for example, if low earnings are due to poor economic conditions). One way to handle this is to group postprogram outcomes by the level of preprogram employment; this would provide a better perspective for interpreting the outcomes. (For evaluating the impacts of specific programs, special studies such as "controlled" experiments are needed.)

Techniques for estimating the unmet need for employment and training services are as yet poorly developed. The statewide household survey on income and employment mentioned earlier can also be used to obtain rough estimates of the need for employment and training programs. In addition, questions can be added to the survey to identify specific skill and educational deficiencies among those unemployed and within low income groups--preferably for various regions of the state as well as the state as a whole.

Uses of Economic Development Outcome Measurements

The purpose of these outcome measurement procedures is to determine the progress of state economic development programs. The information obtained through such procedures provides public officials with a "scorecard" that shows how well their services are achieving major public objectives, both statewide and for varous substate regions and population subgroups (such as different age, sex, or racial groups). As data are obtained over periods of time, time trends can be identified. Such trends should be reviewed as part of the annual budget and planning process. The information should help officials to identify and track problems that appear to merit attention, such as particularly high levels of household unemployment in one region of the state.

Additional uses of outcome information include the following:

(a) With appropriate evaluation designs, it can be used in more detailed program evaluations or analyses on the effectiveness of specific government programs;

(b) It can be used to measure the performance of state employees participating in monetary or other types of incentive programs;

(c) It can be used to control and assess the quality of the performance of a contractor providing economic development services (such as employment and training assistance) to the state government;

(d) It can be used as a quality control check on changes in state programs designed to improve efficiency;

(e) Because of its dependence on information obtained directly from citizens and clients, and because the information obtained can be expressed in terms familiar to citizens, it can serve as an important means of communication in both directions between citizens, clients of economic development activities, and state economic development officials.

Limitations of Economic Development Outcome Measurements

Many of the recommended data collection procedures lack extensive field testing. Furthermore, states that decide to use these procedures are likely to want to alter them somewhat for their own specific needs. Thus, data collection should be preceded by thorough pretesting to insure that reasonably valid and reliable data are being obtained.

In addition, it should be recognized that all outcome measurements of economic development activities have significant limitations at this time.

First, measurement data seldom represent effects due solely to state programs. State programs have limited ability to bring about changes in economic conditions. Success depends to a considerable extent on the government's ability to influence the decisions of private firms and tourists. These private decisions are affected by numerous factors beyond the control of state government. Furthermore, the magnitude of state efforts is often small in relation to other forces in the economy. Measures of a state's overall economy, such as unemployment rates or family/household income, are strongly influenced by external forces. For these reasons, the specific degree of change in outcome data which is attributable to state government efforts can be determined only by in-depth studies, and even then only with difficulty.

Second, some important results of economic development programs will not necessarily appear within one year, the normal time-frame for program monitoring. A state may work with an industrial prospect for several years; tourism promotion may stimulate visits in subsequent travel seasons; or a training program may benefit participants beyond the initial year after their graduation. Thus, outcome data obtained at the end of a given year may not include the full impact of that year's programs and may reflect the effects of programs in previous years.

Finally, it should be noted that economic development programs have secondary effects, such as on tax revenues, residential construction, and consumer spending. The suggested outcome measures do not attempt to measure these secondary outcomes.

Users of the outcome measures recommended in this report should recognize these limitations, since they seem to be unavoidable in regular performance monitoring. Only in-depth, special studies are potentially capable of quantifying the full range of long-term or secondary impacts of economic development programs.

Future Research Needs

Development and testing were limited during the project period. Several issues warrant further research. These include the following:

(1) Testing is needed of the four survey instruments suggested by this report (a statewide survey of households, follow-up surveys of the clients of industrial development services and of tourism services, and a follow-up survey of former participants in employment and training programs). Each survey raises questions of respondents' recall and honesty, and other issues which affect the gathering of accurate and valid data. Testing is desirable to assure that reasonably accurate procedures are used and to determine cost, staffing requirements, and other issues related to feasibility.

(2) As discussed above, most tourism-related employment estimates now focus on total economic impact. Better means of identifying annual changes in employment related to state tourism promotion are needed.

(3) Better methods of defining the unmet need for employment and training programs should be devised. For example, better information on the capacities of the population would aid in defining the need for remedial programs; estimates of the proportion of unemployment related to skill deficiencies might aid in directing training programs.

(4) During the project it was not possible to develop specific criteria for classifying outcome data by case difficulty nor to reflect the influence of external factors. Research into such factors in order to allow better interpretation of the findings on outcomes and how information on them can be presented, would be highly desirable.

Chapter 1

MONITORING PROGRESS TOWARD AGGREGATE ECONOMIC DEVELOPMENT OBJECTIVES

This chapter discusses measures of progress toward aggregate economic development objectives.

The following general objectives for state economic development appear to be generally applicable and are used as the basis for our subsequent suggestions:

Employment

- To maintain or improve utilization of persons who desire work, and
- To maintain or improve the quality of jobs.

Income

- To maintain or improve the ability of families and individuals to purchase their living needs.

Environmental Effects

- To minimize detrimental effects on the environment resulting from economic development, and
- To conserve and utilize energy resources efficiently.

Citizen Satisfaction

- To maximize the satisfaction of citizens with their standard of living.[1]

State governments seek to achieve these overall objectives by such means as industrial development, tourism promotion, and employment and training programs. Measurements of the progress of these three types of programs are the subject of Chapters 2, 3, and 4, respectively. Programs such as education, transportation, and utilities regulation also contribute to economic development, but the programs listed above were selected for consideration because of their immediate relationship to economic development.

---

1. States may want to add other, more specific objectives which reflect their determination to remedy specific economic problems, such as to compensate for declining or cyclical industries or to bolster tax revenues.

Key Measurement Issues

Exhibit 1 lists suggested measures and associated data collection procedures for assessing progress toward overall economic development objectives. This section summarizes the major approaches represented by the measures in the exhibit. The next section discusses the specific measures and associated data collection procedures.

An overview of measures of employment and income (Measures 1 to 7). Estimates of Measure 1 (unemployment rate) are currently available from two sources, the Census Bureau and state bureaus of employment security. Since 1976 the Census Bureau has provided estimates of the average annual unemployment rate for each state and for about thirty of the largest Standard Metropolitan Statistical Areas (SMSA's) and selected central cities. Rates for population subgroups (e.g., by race) are provided only for the largest states, the largest SMSA's, and selected central cities (the subgroup must include a civilian labor force of at least 50,000). These estimates are derived from its regular survey of samples of the nation's population. These are not provided for other counties or substate regions within a state. Only annual average unemployment rates are provided; there are no state or substate estimates released for shorter periods (such as monthly).

State employment security offices use procedures developed by the U.S. Department of Labor to make monthly estimates for states and substate regions but not for other population subgroups. Although these estimates continue to be used for Measure 1, there are questions about their use for assessing year-to-year changes. Both the employment security offices' estimates and (to a lesser degree) those of the Census Bureau involve numerical adjustments to raw data which consist of statewide counts of unemployment insurance claims and responses to the Current Population Survey. These adjustments are based primarily on past relationships and do not seem likely to be sensitive to recent program or policy changes.[1]

Annual per capita income estimates (Measure 6) for states, counties, and SMSA's are made by the Bureau of Economic Analysis (BEA) of the U.S. Department of Commerce.

Measures 2, 3, 4, 5, and 7 are various aspects of employment and income on which reliable annual estimates are not now available for state or substate areas. A statewide survey of a sample of households seems needed to obtain data for these measures. Such a survey offers the additional advantage of providing data that can be disaggregated by major substate regions and population subgroups and provide information on "discouraged workers" and the "dissatisfied part-time employed." The survey could be jointly sponsored by several state agencies to gather data on a variety of services, thereby reducing the cost to each department. The last section of this chapter provides other detailed suggestions for designing, conducting, and using such a survey. The experiences of North Carolina and Wisconsin in conducting tests of similar surveys are also discussed. Appendix A presents an illustrative set of questions for the survey.

-----

1. These problems are discussed in more detail under Measure 1 in the next section.

EXHIBIT 1

SUGGESTED MEASURES OF PROGRESS TOWARD OVERALL ECONOMIC DEVELOPMENT OBJECTIVES

Objective	Suggested Measure	Data Collection or Estimation Procedures
Increase employment/reduce unemployment (of individuals)	1. Rate of unemployment at specific points in time	State employment security agency estimates (state and substate data); state-conducted survey (state and substate data); or U.S. Census Bureau's Current Population Survey (CPS) (statewide annual average only)
	2. Number and percent of the adult labor force plus discouraged workers who experienced unemployment of at least "x" weeks during the past twelve months[a]	State-conducted survey (state and substate data)
Increase employment/reduce unemployment (in households)	3. Number and percent of households which experienced at least "x" weeks during the past twelve months when there was no member employed but at least one member sought work or wanted work but felt it was futile to look for work[a]	State-conducted survey (state and substate data)
Improve job quality	4. Number and percent of the employed population who were working in jobs with wage rates that were less than would be "sufficient" on an annual basis[b]	State-conducted survey (state and substate data)
	5. Number and percent of employed persons who rated the quality of various aspects of their current employment as "fair" or "poor"	State-conducted survey (state and substate data)
Improve personal and household income	6. Per capita income of residents	U.S. Bureau of Economic Analysis estimates (state and substate data)

EXHIBIT 1 (CONT'D)

Objective	Suggested Measure	Data Collection or Estimation Procedures
Improve personal and household income (cont'd)	7. Percent of households with annual incomes of less than "x" dollars (data presented by size of household)[c]	State-conducted survey (state and substate data)
Minimize detrimental effects on the environment	8. Number and percent of days in the previous year that each major water drainage and air basin exceeded maximum air or water pollution limits	State and federal monitoring agencies
	9. Number and percent of industrial sources which exceeded maximum emission standards for at least "x" days in the previous year[d]	State and federal monitoring agencies
Conserve energy resources	10. Number and percent of major industries which exceeded state energy efficiency standards (by type of industry)	State and federal energy agencies
Maintain or increase citizen satisfaction	11. Number and percent of respondents who rated their households' standard of living as "fair" or "poor"	State-conducted survey (state and substate data)
	12. Net migration into or out of the state (and substate regions)	State and federal population estimates (state and substate data)

[a]"x" represents a value, such as four weeks, selected by the state. Data could also be collected on the number of adults or households that are unemployed for various other durations.

[b]"Sufficient" represents a standard defined by reference to the minimum annual income necessary for family or individual support (such as the federally-defined poverty line or a state-defined, low-income line for families of various sizes).

[c]"x" dollars represents a standard, such as the income level necessary to obtain minimum living needs (such as the federally-defined poverty line or a state-defined low-income line).

[d]"x" represents a standard, such as fifteen days.

As an alternative procedure to a state-sponsored survey for estimating duration of individual unemployment, household income and wage sufficiency (Measures 2, 4, and 7), another, as yet untested, procedure merits further exploration. A state government could request that the Census Bureau provide weighted data tabulations from the annual March Current Population Survey (CPS) for the state and substate populations. On the basis of discussions with Census Bureau officials and a review of descriptive information on sampling procedures and questions used in the March CPS, this appears to be an option worth further study by individual states.[1]

It appears that the Census Bureau could provide tabulations for the state as a whole, a set of substate areas chosen so that no one area had less than 250,000 population, and major population subgroups (such as groupings by race or SMSA-nonSMSA). Sample sizes for the March CPS for individual states (including the District of Columbia) currently range from 395 to 5,640. The reliability of estimates for population subgroups will be lower than for statewide totals since they are based on smaller samples.

The following need to be further explored in study of this procedure's feasibility for individual states:

- The extent to which the sample is representative of the particular state and its population subgroups;

- The reliability of estimates from the one-month survey for states with different sample sizes;

- The specific type of data which can be obtained for individual measures; and

- The cost and timing of data obtained using such a procedure.[2]

Measures of the environmental effects of economic development (Measures 8, 9, and 10). Two potentially detrimental effects of economic development should be monitored: environmental damage (Measures 8 and 9) and energy consumption (Measure 10). The former includes air and water pollution, and possibly traffic congestion, noise, and land use. The latter pertains to the energy efficiency

---

1. Only during the March interviews each year are respondents asked about income and duration of employment for the previous year. The primary sources which were used for this and the following information were the March CPS survey instrument, the description of CPS sampling and tabulating procedures in U.S., Department of Labor, Bureau of Labor Statistics, BLS Handbook of Methods for Surveys and Studies, (Washington, D.C., 1976), pp. 5-12, and telephone conversations with two Census Bureau officials who have major responsibilities for the CPS.

2. We also explored the feasibility of a state's adding to the total number of households sampled by the CPS within its borders to increase the representativeness and reliability of estimates for the state as a whole and population subgroups. We identified several potentially major problems which have led us not to recommend this procedure. These included: (1) technical problems

of existing firms and their use of energy resources. These measures focus on existing firms in a region; the assessment of the impacts of only new firms is discussed in Chapters 2 and 3 (measures of industrial development and tourism promotion). Measurement of these effects is included for completeness, but is discussed very briefly as it was not within the scope of this project.

Measures of citizen satisfaction (Measures 11 and 12). Two measures of citizens' satisfaction with their standard of living are included in this chapter:

(a) Expressed satisfaction (Measure 11). In the proposed statewide survey discussed above, citizens would be asked to rate their satisfaction with their standard of living as excellent, good, fair, or poor.

(b) Net migration into or out of the state or substate regions (Measure 12). This measure, which would use existing data, is suggested as indicating a "summation" of many satisfaction-related elements.

Citizen satisfaction data should be gathered for the state as a whole, substate regions, and, where possible, for target population groups. These target groups might be identified by race, sex, age, or educational attainment. For Measure 12, but not Measure 11, comparable data exists on other states. These two measures are more "global" than the others; they do not provide information which can be directly related to specific government activities.

Combining measurement data into summary indices. Summary indices of socio-economic well-being have been suggested by several authors. Levitan and Taggart, for example, have developed an indicator of "employment and earnings inadequacy" which combines unemployment, underemployment, and income data into a single measure pertaining to the functioning of the labor market.[1] Other summary indices have been developed for similar purposes.[2] Some of the components of these summary indices appear as part of measures in this chapter.

---

associated with designing a sample whose responses could be merged with data collected for the national CPS sample; (2) the limited availability of Census Bureau staff to work with state government personnel on such a project, which would probably also mean a very long lead time before this procedure could even be tested; (3) confidentiality restrictions on CPS data; and (4) the probable high costs of such a procedure.

1. Sar A. Levitan and Robert Taggart, "Employment and Earnings Inadequacy: A New Social Indicator," _Challenge_ (January-February 1974), pp. 22ff.

2. For a summary of several indices, see T. Vietorisz, R. Mier, and J. Giblin, "Subemployment: Exclusion and Inadequacy Indexes," _Monthly Labor Review_ (May 1975), pp. 3ff.

Because the emphasis here is on assessing progress toward each of several overall economic development goals, we do not suggest that measures be so combined or weighted unless they can also be reviewed individually.[1]

Individual Measures of Economic Development Objectives

This section contains separate discussions of each of the measures in Exhibit 1.

---

1. Rate of unemployment at specific points in time.

2. Number and percent of the adult labor force plus discouraged workers who experienced unemployment of at least "x" weeks during the past twelve months.

These two related measures indicate the employment status of individuals. Measure 1 pertains to a specific point in time, while Measure 2 pertains to a specific period, such as twelve months. The "x" in Measure 2 represents a value, such as four weeks, selected by the state; data could also be collected for other durations such as "4-13 weeks," "14-26 weeks," "27-39 weeks," and "more than 39 weeks."

The unemployment rate presently used by most states is defined as "the number of unemployed as a percent of the civilian labor force."[2] The civilian labor force includes those who are employed plus those who have ". . . actively looked for work in the past four weeks, are currently available for work, and . . . . do not have a job at the same time."[3] Therefore, the unemployment rate represents the proportion of those in the labor force who want to work and are seeking work but are unable to find employment.

The most frequent criticisms of the unemployment rate as an indicator are that it does not include persons who have given up looking for work (discouraged workers) or persons who hold part-time jobs but wish full-time employment (dissatisfied part-time employed).[4] Data for estimating the size of these two

---

1. Such combinations and weightings imply critical value judgments regarding the importance of individual components. It is our belief that such judgments should be left to the public officials responsible for policy determination. Combinations, however, might be used if desired to illustrate the effects of such weightings.

2. U.S., Department of Labor, Bureau of Labor Statistics, Handbook of Labor Statistics, 1974, Bulletin 1825 (Washington, D.C.: 1974), p. 2.

3. Ibid.

4. Stuart O. Schweitzer and Ralph E. Smith, "The Persistence of the Discouraged Worker Effort," Industrial and Labor Relations Review 27, no. 2 (January 1974); Robert A. Gordon and Margaret S. Gordon, Prosperity and Unemployment (New York: John Wiley and Sons, 1966); Peter Negronida, "Discouraged Worker's Obscure Jobless Picture," Chicago Tribune, 16 June 1975.

groups for individual states are not currently regularly available. As discussed below, a statewide household survey might be used to obtain rough estimates of their size. The survey would need to include questions on why a person is not seeking work or not working full-time.

Measure 2 is intended to provide information on the duration of unemployment of individuals during the past twelve months. Data on this measure are not currently available to states. Procedures for estimating it from household survey data are described below.

Employment security agencies currently estimate the average length of time since a worker was last employed, based primarily on unemployment compensation reports. These data, however, do not include persons who are not eligible for benefits or otherwise do not claim unemployment benefits. Measure 2 seeks to estimate duration of unemployment among all individuals in the work force or who wanted work but felt it was futile to look for work, including persons not eligible or otherwise not claiming unemployment benefits. As such, data are not presently collected on this measure.[1]

Data Collection Procedures for Measure 1

For 1976 and later years, state governments will be able to obtain estimated average annual unemployment rates (as traditionally defined) for the state as a whole from the U.S. Bureau of Labor Statistics (BLS). Estimating such rates for all states using CPS data is a new procedure recently initiated to secure statistics for use in allocating federal Comprehensive Employment and Training Act (CETA) funds. These estimates will be published by BLS in the spring following the year for which they have been calculated.[2] The Census Bureau estimates that with their current state sample sizes chances are two out of three that average annual unemployment rates for states are at least within 10 percent of the rates that would be reported by a full census count (they are more accurate for many states with larger sample sizes). Since the CPS was originally designed to secure data for making national estimates, some questions arise concerning the use of CPS data to make state estimates. States using the BLS estimates for outcome monitoring should explore the sampling and statistical adjustment procedures used by the Census Bureau for any features which might cause estimates for their states to be unrepresentative of the state's population or insensitive to program or policy changes because of statistical adjustment procedures used.

---

1. In 1977, the Bureau of Labor Statistics for the first time published estimated annual averages for duration of unemployment in twenty-six states and twenty-nine SMSA's. Duration of unemployment was defined as the average length of time since a worker was last employed. Estimates were provided for 1975, based on responses to the monthly CPS in 1975. U.S., Department of Labor, Bureau of Labor Statistics, Geographic Profile of Employment and Unemployment, 1975, BLS Report 481 (Washington, D.C., 1977).

2. For earlier years (beginning in 1971), estimated annual averages for the nineteen largest states and the thirty largest SMSA's only were published in the BLS series called Geographic Profile of Employment and Unemployment.

Monthly data on unemployment rates for states and substate regions are available at no cost to the state from state employment security agencies. Similar data exist on other states, permitting comparisons with other states and the nation as a whole.

Employment security unemployment estimates are obtained using the procedures known as the "seventy-step method" devised by BLS.[1] These data are based on the number of unemployment compensation claims plus estimates of the number of unemployed persons who, though eligible, are not claiming unemployment insurance benefits and those who are not eligible for benefits because they have exhausted eligibility or did not have previous insured employment. States should note that these adjustment procedures can affect the accuracy of such estimates.

Beginning in 1973, the U.S. Department of Labor adopted several changes aimed at improving the validity of its estimation procedures. These included basing unemployment estimates on place of worker's residence rather than place of employment and modifying state unemployment rates, by using data from the CPS to achieve interstate uniformity.[2] Despite these changes, the accuracy of these estimates is still in doubt. In 1975, for example, a study of unemployment in St. Louis was conducted in which labor force data were collected by a survey which utilized methods, definitions, and procedures similar to those used by the Census Bureau for the CPS. The St. Louis survey was based on personal interviews of about 1,500 randomly selected households in each of three months; completion rates ranged from 94.1 percent to 96.6 percent. The resulting data varied widely from data collected by the state employment security agency. For the three months of the study, citywide unemployment was found to be 19.2 percent, 16.3 percent and 15.1 percent by the survey, compared to 11.8 percent, 11.9 percent and 11.4 percent found by the state employment security agency. The study concluded that the seventy-step method has inaccuracies when used to estimate unemployment for substate areas because:

(a) The size of certain demographic groups, especially those which are most mobile and most difficult to locate, is underestimated.

(b) The accuracy and completeness of employment security agency records may vary greatly among local offices.

(c) The actual operation of local labor markets may not coincide with assumptions of the seventy-step method about national labor market behavior.[3]

As to the use of statewide household surveys, initially the survey's most important uses will probably be to provide rough estimates of two

1. U.S., Department of Labor, Bureau of Labor Statistics, BLS Handbook of Methods, pp. 62-65.

2. James R. Wetzel and Martin Ziegler, "Measuring Unemployment in States and Local Areas," Monthly Labor Review (June 1974), pp. 40ff.

3. University of Missouri-St. Louis, Extension Division, Measuring Unemployment in the City of St. Louis, (St. Louis, December 1975). See also J.W.D. Noviski, "Millions of Dollars in Federal Aid Given Localities on Inaccurate Data," Washington Post, 14 April 1975, p. C-1.

unemployment statistics not otherwise available--the numbers of discouraged workers and dissatisfied part-time workers who are available for full-time work.

Discouraged workers would include all individuals who are able to work and wanted work, but felt it was futile to look for work. They could be identified by the household survey as all individuals for whom one of the first four reasons for not looking for work was given as the major reason in response to Question 14 in Appendix A.

A modification of the traditional unemployment rate which includes discouraged workers could thus be calculated from the household survey by adding this number of discouraged workers to those not employed but seeking work ("yes" responses to Question 13), and dividing this sum by the number in the labor force (the unemployed identified by "yes" responses to Question 13 plus persons identified by "employed" or "employed but not at work" answers to Question 7) plus discouraged workers.[1]

No measure is included in Exhibit 1 to identify the number of dissatisfied part-time employed workers--individuals who, though presently employed part-time, would like to work full-time. Such information can be obtained if the statewide household survey is undertaken. They might be identified through the household survey using questions such as 8, 9, and 10 in Appendix A. More detailed information on why the individual was not working full-time (such as "family responsibilities/child care" or "lack of transportation") could also be obtained by using a question such as 11 in Appendix A.

Results of the 1976 test survey in North Carolina contained very few "don't know" responses for questions in Appendix A which would be used to estimate unemployment rates from responses for all adult household members (respondents and other adults). The accuracy of the respondent's information regarding other household members was, however, not tested.

In the North Carolina test, for approximately 3 percent of the adults (respondents and other adult household members) who were reported as employed, "don't know" responses were given to a subsequent question about how many hours the individual had worked last week. This made it difficult to obtain an accurate estimate of the number of dissatisfied part-time workers. In the 1976 test survey in Wisconsin, "don't know" responses for a question on how many hours employed adults had worked last week were a lower proportion, about 1 percent of respondents and other adults employed. Also in Wisconsin, the "don't know" rate for a subsequent question on the reason for working less than 35 hours the previous week was very low, about 0.2 percent of the total of respondents and other household adults who worked less than 35 hours.

---

1. In order for the state household survey recommended in this report to be a source of accurate estimates of unemployment rates, discouraged workers, or dissatisfied part-time workers, the sample of all adults in a random sample of state households would need to approximate a random sample of state adults. See more discussion of this issue later in this chapter under "Survey Design and Costs."

Data Collection Procedures for Measure 2

Measure 2 requires data not presently available from existing state or federal sources. The household survey appears to be the best source of data for this measure.

Questions 4 through 6 in Appendix A identify individuals who experienced unemployment during the previous twelve months and reasons for the unemployment.

To obtain Measure 2, the number of individuals with a total of "x" or more weeks in which they were either unemployed and seeking work (Question 6, Item a) or discouraged (Question 6, Item d, "no work, futile to look") would be divided by the sum of the number in the labor force ("yes" responses to Question 13 plus "employed" or "employed but not at work" answers to Question 7) plus discouraged workers (one of the first four reasons given as the major reason for not seeking work in response to Question 14).[1]

These questions rely on reasonably accurate reporting by respondents of the length of unemployment periods of both the respondent and other household members for the past twelve months. The Continuous Longitudinal Manpower Survey (CLMS) of the Department of Labor has obtained work history for periods greater than twelve months, but only on the respondent.[2] The ability of questions such as those in Appendix A to gather reliable data on the work history of both the respondent and other household members remains to be determined.

---

3. Number and percent of households which experienced at least "x" weeks during the past twelve months when there was no member employed but at least one member sought work or wanted work but felt it was futile to look for work.

Whereas Measure 1 and 2 focus on the individual worker, Measure 3 focuses on the household and on periods during which no member of the household is employed. These are periods of particular hardship to the household. Unemployment can adversely affect household units by causing loss of income and social instability. Measure 3 identifies the existence of periods in which the household did not contain at least one employed person even though at least one member wanted to work. Periods when no members wanted work are excluded, so the measure does not include planned periods of nonemployment, such as retirement. Data on Measure 3 are not currently collected by federal or state agencies. We recommend this measure as a complement to the measures of unemployment of individuals.

---

1. In order for the state household survey recommended in this report to be a source of accurate estimates of duration of individual unemployment, the sample of all adults in a random sample of state households would need to approximate a random sample of state adults. See more discussion of this issue later in this chapter under "Survey Design and Costs."

2. Westat, Inc., Continuous Longitudinal Manpower Survey Characteristics of CETA Participants Enrolled During Third Quarter of FY 1975, Report No. 1 (Washington, D.C.: U.S. Department of Labor, Employment and Training Administration, Office of Program Evaluation, January 1976), p. 4-1.

"Household" rather than the "family" seems appropriate as the unit of analysis for Measure 3 (and Measure 7 below).[1] This unit does not exclude state households not related by blood, marriage, or adoption as a family unit would. The disadvantage of "household" is that in some cases household members may not be interdependent in terms of income or expenditures.

Some states, however, may choose to use the family as the unit of analysis so that the measure will be comparable with other statistics collected by the state. It was for this reason--and also to be compatible with federal usage--that "family" was chosen for the Wisconsin survey. "Household" was used in North Carolina.

In the wording of the measure, "x" represents a value, such as four weeks, selected by the state. Data could also be grouped into ranges, such as "none," "less than 4 weeks," "4-13 weeks," "14-26 weeks," "27-39 weeks," and "more than 39 weeks."

Data Collection Procedures

Data for this measure would be collected by means of the statewide household survey. Questions 2 and 3 in Appendix A are designed to gather the data. To obtain the percentage for Measure 3, the number of responses of "x" or more weeks to Question 3 would be divided by the total of "yes" and "no" responses to Question 2.

This measure is subject to error due to inaccurate recall by the respondent of unemployment status of household members. (These problems were discussed in connection with Measure 2.) In the Wisconsin survey, "don't know" or "don't remember" was given by respondents on _duration_ of unemployment for about 4 percent of the families which had experienced periods in the previous year when at least one immediate family member was seeking work but no immediate family member was employed.[2]

---

4. Number and percent of the employed population who were working in jobs with wage rates that were less than would be "sufficient" on an annual basis.

5. Number and percent of employed persons who rated the quality of various aspects of their current employment as "fair" or "poor."

---

1. The U.S. Department of Commerce defines "family" as a group composed of two or more persons who are ". . . . related by blood, marriage, or adoption . . . ." and a "household" as including ". . . . all persons who occupy a group of rooms or a single room that constitutes a housing unit . . . ." (U.S., Department of Commerce, Social and Economic Statistics Administration, _Dictionary of Economic and Statistical Terms_ [Washington, D.C., November 1972], p. 62.)

2. The question in the Wisconsin survey did not include any mention of a family member who "wanted work but felt it was futile to look for work" as we recommend for Measure 3.

In addition to employment status, there are other aspects of employment that are of major importance to citizens. These include such factors as adequacy of income, stability of employment, opportunities for advancement, skill level utilized, and working conditions.[1] These aspects can be influenced by state economic development efforts. For example, industrial promotion can influence the types of firms that move into the state and employment and training programs can raise the skill level of the work force.

Measure 4 indicates the proportion of employed persons who held jobs paying wages that, on a full-time annual basis, would be insufficient for family support. It is similar to Measure 7, but the latter focuses on total family/household income. Measure 5 requires the state to define a minimum standard of wage "sufficiency." This should probably be the wage that would yield annual earnings sufficient to support an average-size household.

The federal low-income standard discussed in Measure 7 (or perhaps a somewhat greater amount) might be a suitable standard of income sufficiency. Two problems arise in defining an independent standard:

(a) Estimating sufficiency on the basis of the current wage rate projected to an annual amount does not identify jobs which are seasonal and yield insufficient wages.

(b) A sufficiency standard based on family needs may overestimate the income needs of single individuals or families with more than one wage earner. Some studies have approached this problem by using different standards for judging the wages of primary and secondary wage earners.[2]

These two problems can be reduced by gathering data on employment characteristics (temporary or seasonal) and family role (primary or secondary wage earner). Due to the complexity this would add to data collection, however, such refinements should probably be reserved for special studies.

Measure 5 is included to represent employed persons' perceptions of key characteristics of their work. It considers such aspects of job quality as adequacy of earnings, opportunities for advancement, utilization of skills, quality of working conditions, and overall satisfaction with present job.

Data Collection Procedures

Measures 4 and 5 both use data obtained by the statewide household survey. For Measure 4, an alternative procedure, discussed earlier in this chapter

---

1. Job quality has been frequently discussed in literature describing subemployment and secondary labor markets. See William Springer, Bennett Harrison, and Thomas Vietorisz, "Crisis of the Underemployed," New York Times Magazine, 5 November 1972; Sar A. Levitan and Robert Taggart, "Employment-Earnings Inadequacy: A Measure of Welfare," Monthly Labor Review (October 1973); Herman P. Miller, "Sub-Employment in Poverty Areas of Large U.S. Cities," Monthly Labor Review (October 1973). See also Vietorisz, Mier, and Giblin, "Subemployment," pp. 3-12.

2. See Springer, Harrison and Vietorisz, "Crisis."

also merits further exploration by individual states. It would involve state requests to the Census Bureau for unpublished estimates for the state and state population subgroups based on March CPS data.

Question 12 on the illustrative questionnaire in Appendix A is designed to gather data on present wage level for use in calculating Measure 4. As shown in Question 12, the interviewer would calculate the annual equivalent of the wage level reported by the respondent for each adult member of the household.[1] This annual equivalent would subsequently be compared with the state's "sufficiency" standard to determine whether each individual was above or below the standard.[2]

Measure 5 would utilize data obtained from Question 15 to obtain respondents' perceptions of selected aspects of their current jobs.[3] The survey approach suggested involves interviewing any available adult household member (but only one adult in each household), regardless of whether the respondent is employed. Question 15 is to be asked only of employed respondents. Thus, if the number of respondents who are employed is low, there will be few responses to Question 15. The times of interviewing should include evening and weekend hours to reach a reasonable proportion of working adults.

The North Carolina survey asked each employed respondent to rate specific aspects of his or her current job, including its opportunity for advancement, safety, use of skills, and likelihood of steady employment. Of 1,385 completed interviews, 62 percent (859) involved respondents who were qualified to respond to the questions for Measure 5.

---

6. Per capita income of residents.[4]

---

1. In order for the state household survey recommended in this report to be a source of accurate estimates of wage sufficiency, the sample of all employed adults in a random sample of state households would need to approximate a random sample of employed adults in the state. See more discussion of this issue later in this chapter under "Survey Design and Costs."

2. Average state wage levels are computed annually for several occupational and industrial categories covered by unemployment insurance. These were considered as a possible alternative source of data for Measure 4, but they do not include some important groups of workers and they do not allow tabulation of the number of jobs below a "sufficiency" standard.

3. In order for the state household survey recommended in this report to be a source of accurate estimates of job quality in the state, the sample of employed respondents in a random sample of state households would need to approximate a random sample of employed persons in the state. See more discussion of this issue later in this chapter under "Survey Design and Costs."

4. "Total personal income" and "gross state product" are sometimes used as measures of economic development. They are not suggested here because they make no allowance for population changes and therefore do not reflect individual well-being.

Per capita income is total personal income in an area divided by population. While per capita income is an appropriate general indicator of economic well-being, it has three important deficiencies as an economic development outcome measure:

(a) It does not show changes in the distribution of income among population groups. For example, overall per capita income may increase while the per capita income of certain population groups improves to a lesser degree or decreases. Also, because per capita income is influenced by income extremes, data on areas with major disparities in income levels may be misleading.[1]

(b) It does not distinguish income received from public assistance from other types of personal income.

(c) As with all income measures in this chapter, it does not make allowances for the wealth held by individuals or for changes in individual wealth over time, except insofar as wealth generates personal income.

An advantage of using per capita income is that comparable data are available for all counties in the United States and over a period of years. When these comparisons are made, differences in price levels (cost of living) should be taken into account. The following are three approaches which might be used to make the desirable adjustments:

(1) Adjust state per capita income by the national Consumer Price Index (CPI).

(2) Adjust state per capita income by a state consumer price index.[2]

(3) State Measure 6 in a slightly different form: ratio of state per capita income (unadjusted) to national or another state per capita income (unadjusted). This seems particularly appropriate for comparisons between states.

As with other measures, the precise form of this measure may be adapted to reflect particular state objectives. For example, North Carolina has set forth these economic development goals: to "close the gap in income which exists between North Carolina and the nation (and) to establish and maintain

---

1. U.S., Department of Commerce, Economic Development Administration, Developing Methodologies for Evaluating the Impact of EDA Programs (Washington, D.C., January 1972), p. 4.

2. The North Carolina Department of Administration, for example, is developing a state-specific consumer price index. At the present time it includes indexes on food, restaurant meals, home ownership, fuel and utilities, public transportation, and motels and hotels. Data are collected twice yearly from most areas across the state. Indexes are computed for the state, urban North Carolina, rural North Carolina, and Mountain, Piedmont, and Coastal areas. For further discussion, see a recent issue of Cost of Living Indicators (Raleigh, N.C.: Office of State Department of Administration).

North Carolina as a regional leader in income . . . ." Measures of progress toward these goals could be stated as:

(a) State per capita income as a percent of per capita income for the nation and for the thirteen southeastern states; or

(b) Rank of the state in level of per capita income among all states in the nation and the thirteen southeastern states.

Data Collection Procedures

Per capita income data are published by the Bureau of Economic Analysis (BEA) of the U.S. Department of Commerce.[1] These estimates are made annually for each state, county, and Standard Metropolitan Statistical Area (SMSA).

Preliminary state estimates are usually available in April for the previous calendar year. They are published in the April issue of the Survey of Current Business (a monthly BEA publication which usually comes out about the second week of May). Revised state estimates are published in the August issue of the Survey.

County and SMSA estimates are available about a year later than state estimates. They are also published in the April issue of the Survey for the calendar year two years previous. No revised estimates are published.

County data are available for selected years between 1920 and 1962 and annually beginning with 1965. No breakdowns by demographic group are made at

---

1. The Census Bureau has also recently developed another procedure for calculating per capita income estimates for states, counties, and other incorporated places. The primary use of these estimates has been in allocating federal funds among state and local governments. The procedures were instituted in response to needs generated by the federal, general revenue-sharing program which began in 1972.

The Census estimates are based on several sources, including 1970 census data on income and related areas, federal income tax returns, special studies, and the BEA per capita income estimates discussed in this section. There are some differences in income definitions and coverage between the BEA and Census Bureau estimates.

Since Census Bureau estimates for any calendar year are available about one year later than BEA estimates for states and about two years later than BEA estimates for substate areas, the BEA estimates are probably preferable for annual outcome monitoring.

States interested in more information on the Census Bureau estimates should consult U.S., Census Bureau, Current Population Reports Series P-25, nos. 649 to 698 (Washington, D.C., 1977). In this series, there is a separate issue for each state (for example, no. 649 is Alabama) which includes 1974 per capita income estimates for the state and all of the state's counties and incorporated places. Each issue also includes a general discussion of the methodology used to derive the estimates.

the county or state level, however, and it is not possible to compute these
from the raw data.[1]

BEA computations are based on state and federal data collected from unemployment and social security agencies, and private sources such as the American
Hospital Association and the Association of American Railroads. Approximately
325 income items are included in the calculations. BEA estimates include
several nonmoney income items, such as net rental value of owner-occupied homes
and the value of food and fuel produced on farms. Military personnel and prison
inmates are included in the income and population estimates.

BEA per capita income estimates are subject to potential errors in com-
puting both income and population. For example, to calculate total transfer
payments as one general element of income, forty-five separate data series
are necessary. About one-half of these use data directly from government
records (such as social security payments to individuals). The other half make
indirect use of data in the records; for example, records of total payments
to veterans are allocated equally among the total veteran population.[2] The
total population of the nation, state, or county is derived from estimates made
by the Federal-State Cooperative Program, which is discussed below under Measure
12.

---

7. Percent of households with annual incomes of less than "x" dollars
(data presented by size of household).

Household income probably reflects economic well-being better than per
capita income does. As noted earlier, per capita income is an overall average
for all persons and does not in any way provide information on how it is distributed among individuals, families, or households. Also, the household provides
a better unit to use in assessing the adequacy of incomes because (a) the household represents an economic unit which may receive income contributed by several
members, and (b) the adequacy of income is in part a function of the number of
persons that income is expected to support.

Here, as in Measure 3, we recommend that a state use the "household" rather
than the "family" as the unit of analysis. This unit does not exclude state
households not related by blood, marriage, or adoption as a family unit would.
A disadvantage of "household" (as mentioned earlier) is that its members may
not be interdependent in terms of income or expenditures. Another possible
disadvantage is that since federal low-income or poverty standards are defined
for family units, direct application of those standards to household income
may contain some degree of error.

The basic purpose of Measure 7 is to show the proportion of the population
receiving income which is insufficient to provide for basic living needs. The

---

1. "County and Metropolitan Area Personal Income," Survey of Current
Business 55, no. 4 (April 1975), pp. 30-32.

2. Ibid., p. 32.

value "x" in the measure is a set of minimum standards representing the amount
of income needed to pay for the basic living expenses of households of various
sizes. This set of standards could be adapted from the federal low-income
standard, or poverty line, which takes into account the number and age of family
members and the sex of the head of the household. If the federally-defined
standard is used, the standard should be adjusted to reflect differences in the
state's cost of living, which some states are beginning to identify.

Measure 7 should probably be calculated in two forms. The first would
include income from all sources, both public and private. The second would
include income from all sources except public assistance. The importance of
the latter is that it shows the degree to which the private economic system is
providing for household needs.[1] The former shows how well living needs are being
met with the assistance of transfer payments, which are intended to compensate
for private economic conditions.

In the measure of total income from public and private sources, we assume
that money from three general sources would be included: (1) wages, salaries,
or earnings from self-employment; (2) interest, dividends, rents, alimony or
child support, and pensions; and (3) transfer payments, such as unemployment compensation, welfare, and social security.[2] This approach will probably be sufficient for monitoring general economic conditions, but it does have some limitations.
It is based on money income alone, and so does not consider wealth or "in-kind"
income. A household which owns its own home or has a garden in which it raises
much of its own food will not require as much income to meet "minimum living
needs" as will one which rents housing or is paying off a mortgage, or buys all
of its food.[3]

Deciding on the types of transfer payments to exclude from the second form
of Measure 7 is not simple. It is probably advisable to exclude the major categories of public assistance generally related to low income or lack of work,
such as unemployment compensation, food stamps, aid to families with dependent
children, and supplementary security income.

As with per capita income data, household income data should be adjusted
to account for the effects of price changes when year-to-year changes are
analyzed.

---

1. The extent to which national estimates for these two forms of a "poverty"
measure show significantly different conditions and trends is documented and
discussed in a recent study by the Congressional Budget Office. See U.S.,
Congressional Budget Office, Poverty Status of Families Under Alternative
Definitions of Income, Background Paper no. 17 (Washington, D.C., 13 January
1977).

2. In the Current Population Survey, information on income is collected and
reported in eight categories: money wages and salary; net income from nonfarm
self-employment; net income from farm self-employment; social security; dividends,
interest, royalties, and net rental income; public assistance payments; unemployment compensation, veterans payments, and workman's compensation; and private
pensions, annuities, alimony, and other periodic income.

3. The federal government has taken into account the different living
situation of farm families by defining different "low income standards" for farm
and nonfarm families. A similar adjustment might be made in setting a value
for "x" for use in calculating Measure 7.

Measure 7 is sometimes referred to as a measure of income distribution. We are not recommending any other measures related to income distribution as a part of a state's annual monitoring efforts because the distribution of income is not likely to change rapidly enough to make additional annual monitoring useful.[1]

Data collected for Measure 7 could also be used to show how household income in the state and substate regions was distributed. For example, measurement data could be stated as the percentage of all households with incomes in each of the following ranges: "below $5,000"; "$5,000 to 10,000"; "$10,000 to 15,000"; and "over $15,000."

Data Collection Procedures

The Bureau of Economic Analysis does not provide annual estimates of household or family income as it does per capita income. We recommend that data for calculating this measure be obtained from the statewide household survey. An alternative procedure, discussed earlier in this chapter but as yet untested, also merits further exploration by individual states. It would involve state requests for unpublished estimates for the state and state population subgroups based on March CPS data.

Questions 16 through 21 in Appendix A are designed to gather household income data. Question 16 asks the respondent to estimate the gross wages or salaries earned by each household member. Questions 17 through 21 ask the respondent to estimate various nonwage or salary types of income received by members of the household. This approach is similar to that used by the Census Bureau's CPS each March. Its use requires careful training of interviewers and proper testing of questions.

Several issues deserve further testing to insure the reliability of household income data gathered by a state-sponsored household survey. In the North Carolina test, inerviewers received "don't know" responses on household income from approximately 25 percent (356 of 1,385) of those interviewed. In Wisconsin, the nonresponse rate was 29 percent for a similar question. These rates are

---

1. For example, another type of measure of income distribution is represented by the "Gini Coefficient." This is a mathematical formulation which state policy makers may find difficult to understand. A simpler approach is to use "income shares," the proportion of total income received by each one-fifth of the population or households. The percentage of total income received by each fifth of U.S. families and unrelated individuals varied between 1947 and 1970 in the following ranges of percentage shares: lowest fifth, 3.1 percent to 3.8 percent; second fifth, 10.2 percent to 10.7 percent; third fifth, 16.7 percent to 17.5 percent; fourth fifth, 23.6 percent to 24.8 percent; highest fifth, 43.4 percent to 45.6 percent. U.S., Department of Commerce, Bureau of Census, Historical Statistics of the United States (Washington, D.C., September 1975), p. 292. 1975), p. 292.
For a review of alternate measures of income distribution, see Joseph L. Gastworth, "The Estimation of the Lorenz Curve and Gini Index," Review of Economics and Statistics (August 1972), pp. 306-16.

both higher than the 19 percent nonresponse rate the Census Bureau has obtained recently.[1] The cause of these rates of nonresponse is uncertain, but they pose a possible important source of error. Further testing of income questions and investigation of the reasons for nonresponse is needed, with particular attention to how nonresponses are affecting the two forms of the measure of low-income households recommended here (one with and one without public assistance income).

Another possible source of error is that the relative difficulty of locating low-income households may cause underestimation of the lowest income group. Efforts made in Wisconsin and North Carolina to deal with this problem are discussed later.

---

8. Number and percent of days in the previous year that each major water drainage and air basin exceeded maximum air or water pollution limits.

9. Number and percent of industrial sources which exceeded maximum emission standards for at least "x" days in the previous year.

Most state governments and the federal government have set minimum standards for environmental quality and have undertaken programs to monitor compliance with these standards.[2] In the measure, "x" represents a preselected value such as fifteen days. In monitoring state economic development, explicit consideration should be given to the possible detrimental effects of existing industry on the environment.

The purpose of these two measures is to monitor the severity of detrimental environmental effects due to industrial activity. These measures focus on industrial sources because economic development programs usually attempt to increase the level of industrial activity. (Here we are using the term "industrial" to refer to manufacturing and processing operations, rather than the more general use noted in the discussion of "industrial" development in Chapter 2.) Other measures would need to be developed for measuring the effects of other economic activities, such as the effect of increased tourism on air quality.

Measure 8 indicates the progress made in maintaining or reducing air and water pollution levels in major areas of the state. Since air and water pollution standards generally apply to overall pollution levels regardless of source, the state want want to focus more specifically on pollutants produced by industrial sources.

---

1. U.S., Department of Commerce, Bureau of the Census, "Money Income in 1973 of Families and Persons in the United States," Current Population Reports, Consumer Income Series P-60, no. 97 (Washington, D.C., January 1975), p. 177.

2. Some of the difficulties in setting and maintaining air and water pollution standards are discussed in annual reports of the U.S. Council on Environmental Quality published by the Government Printing Office.

Measure 9 is based on data on air and water pollution at their sources. To conserve data collection resources, we recommend that the state collect data only on major industrial sources. Extensive technology is being developed to monitor compliance with environmental standards, but discussion of these data collection procedures is beyond the scope of this report.

Note that these measures would pertain to existing firms. The "existing" firms should not exclude "new" firms, e.g., firms in the first year of operation. The environmental impact of only new firms is discussed in Chapter 2.

---

10. Number and percent of major industries which exceeded state energy efficiency standards (by type of industry).

Energy costs, the efficiency of energy utilization, and conservation are increasingly important to states and to the federal government. State objectives regarding energy use are still only vaguely defined, and in many cases the necessary measurement technologies have not been developed.

Measure 10 presumes the existence of energy efficiency standards. These do not exist in most states as yet. They might be formulated by reference to national industrial averages or standards of energy consumed per unit of output.

Energy production and conservation technology and measurement techniques are developing very rapidly. Therefore, Measure 10 indicates the likely format of such a measure. More precise definition of the measure and discussion of data collection procedures is probably premature and is beyond the scope of this project.

This measure also would pertain to existing firms. The impact of only new firms might also be considered, as discussed in Chapter 2.

---

11. Number and percent of respondents who rated their households' standard of living as "fair" or "poor."

Employment, income, and other statistics on economic conditions do not necessarily indicate citizens' perceptions of their standard of living. Thus, citizens' satisfaction with their economic situation should probably be considered a separate measure of economic conditions.[1]

Measure 11 is based on data on the current level of satisfaction. A variation of this measure would be the number and percent of respondents who rate their households' present standard of living as much better, somewhat better,

---

1. General "quality of life" might also be used, but the measure used here is intended to focus more narrowly on factors related to economic well-being. For a discussion of a quality of life indicator which includes several socioeconomic criteria, see Ben-Chieh Liv, "Quality of Life: Concept, Measure, and Results," American Journal of Economics and Sociology 34, no. 1 (January 1975), p. 1.

somewhat worse, or much worse than one year ago. This variation does not by itself indicate the level of satisfaction but does indicate respondents' feelings as to whether conditions are improving or worsening. Both measures might be used.

Data Collection Procedures

The statewide survey of households can be used to collect data on this measure. Question 22 (and Question 23 for the variation) in Appendix A could be used to gather data for these measures. These questions might be followed by an open-ended question or several specific questions to probe the respondents' reasons for their ratings, especially where the respondents replied "poor."

The North Carolina survey asked for an overall rating of the household's standard of living, a rating of the present standard with that of a year ago, and ratings of individual factors, such as availability of job opportunities. Other factors such as the level of taxes and the cost of living, could also be rated. By obtaining more specific responses, the state might be able to assess, at least roughly, the extent to which its policies have affected or might affect the overall ratings.

It is difficult to assess the validity of this measure without elaborate psychological testing. There is however, extensive experience using perception questions. If the wording of the question is reasonably clear and unambiguous and the interviewing is done properly, responses seem to be a reasonably accurate reflection of how the respondent feels at the time of questioning.

---

12. Net migration into or out of the state (and substate regions).[1]

The movement of people into and out of an area appears to be heavily influenced by economic conditions.[2] Movements among substate regions may help to identify the relative attractiveness of regions from the standpoint of the people who live there.[3] Migration is therefore suggested as a second indicator of citizen satisfaction.

Economic conditions are, of course, not the only factors which influence migration.[4] Migration data from several years should be compared with other

---

1. A variation of Measure 12 is "net migration into or out of the state (and substate regions) as a percent of the total state (regional) population."

2. Richard F. Wertheimer II, The Monetary Rewards of Migration Within the U.S. (Washington, D.C.: The Urban Institute, 1970), and Julie DaVanzo, An Analytical Framework for Studying the Potential Effects of an Income Maintenance Program on U.S. Interregional Migration (Santa Monica, Calif.: Rand Corporation, December 1972).

3. C. Horace Hamilton, North Carolina Population Trends (Chapel Hill: Carolina Population Center, University of North Carolina, 1974).

4. Wertheimer, The Monetary Rewards.

measures of economic conditions and data on citizens' satisfaction with their
standard of living (Measure 11).[1] Where major inconsistencies among these
data persist over several years, it is likely that other motivating factors
are stronger than economic conditions.

Migration out of the state, or out of substate regions with poor economic
conditions, rather than being undesirable, may actually be part of the remedy
for chronically depressed areas.[2]

Data Collection Procedures

State governments cooperate with the Census Bureau annually to update
population statistics from the decennial census on states, counties, and major
cities. These are general population estimates that are not broken down by
demographic characteristics. The accuracy of these estimates was tested recently by the Census Bureau for 1970. It was found that the procedures yielded
differences averaging about 1.85 percent at the state level, and about 4.5 percent for county estimates when compared to 1970 census data.[3]

For analytical purposes, it is desirable that the personal characteristics
of persons leaving and entering a state or region be identified. Age, race, and
educational level seem to be particularly significant.[4] Because the net migration data compiled by the Census Bureau do not contain such information, we
suggest two sources that can provide information on new arrivals only.

The state household survey could gather data on new residents using questions 24 through 26 in Appendix A. These questions would obtain information on
the duration of residence at the respondent's present address and, where duration
was less than twelve months, the location of previous residence. Disaggregation
of these data by population group or region, while feasible, would add to survey
costs.

---

1. Muller cites several examples of situations where net migration may appear
to be inconsistent with other indicators: (a) in areas of rapidly expanding
employment, unemployment may be high at the same time that in-migration is high
(e.g., Alaska), and (b) mild climates and amenities may attract population to
areas in spite of high unemployment levels (e.g., San Diego and San Francisco).
Thomas Muller, Economic Impacts of Land Development: Employment, Housing, and
Property Values (Washington, D.C.: The Urban Institute, 1976).

2. DaVanzo, An Analytical Framework.

3. It has been estimated that new procedures developed for use in the 1970's
would have reduced the average difference in state estimates in 1970 to 1.2
percent. U.S., Bureau of the Census, "1973 Population and 1972 Per Capita Income
Estimates for Counties and Incorporated Places in North Carolina," Current
Population Reports Series P-25, no. 578 (Washington, D.C., May 1975), p. v.

4. U.S., Bureau of the Census, "Mobility of the Population of the United
States: March 1970 to March 1974," Current Population Reports Series P-20,
no. 273 (Washington, D.C., 1974).

The Current Population Survey also makes available data on the characteristics of state households which have lived at their present address for less than five years, at a cost of about $5,000.[1] These data, however, are not representative of most states or of most substate regions. The delay in obtaining this information is somewhat greater than the twelve to eighteen month delay (from the date of a particular survey) for obtaining other types of CPS data by special order.[2]

Both CPS and state survey data pertain only to new residents. Neither source can be used to identify the characteristics of persons who have left a state or region.

The Statewide Household Survey

Measures 2, 3, 4, 5, 7, and 11 rely on data from a state government-sponsored survey of households. Measures 1 and 6 can also be calculated from responses to such a survey, but we recommend estimates based on existing sources. (Estimates based on survey responses are also recommended for checking and refining the estimates from the other sources for Measure 1, as discussed above.)

The household survey is needed to gather data not available from existing sources, to disaggregate data on population subgroups and substate regions, and to obtain data on citizen perceptions.

The sections which follow discuss (1) survey design and costs, (2) a survey instrument, (3) presenting and interpreting survey results, and (4) coordinating the survey and its uses.[3] Exhibit 2 summarizes the major characteristics of the proposed statewide household survey.

Survey Design and Costs

Three general interviewing methods can be used in a state household survey: in-person, telephone, or mail. A combination of these methods appears feasible and appropriate to keep down costs of the survey while avoiding large potential

---

1. U.S., Bureau of the Census, Microdata from the Current Population Survey: The Annual Demographic File, DAD no. 37 (Washington, D.C., December 1974).

2. Personal communications, members of CPS Section, U.S. Bureau of the Census, 1975 and 1976.

3. A number of the issues for such a household survey are discussed in North Carolina, Division of State Budget and Management, Department of Administration, How the Survey Was Conducted and What It Cost (Raleigh, May 1977). This discusses the experiences with the 1976 North Carolina statewide citizen survey which queried citizens on employment and earnings as well as on other state services such as health. For a presentation of how part of the data was presented, see two other volumes in the same North Carolina, Division of State Budget and Management, Department of Administration, series: How Well Off Are North Carolinians? and Guide to the Use of Economic Effectiveness Measurements (Raleigh, May 1977).

EXHIBIT 2

CHARACTERISTICS OF PROPOSED STATEWIDE HOUSEHOLD SURVEY

General Description:

A questionnaire similar to Appendix A would be administered annually to a sample of 1,500 to 2,000 households to obtain data on the employment, income, and citizen satisfaction measures presented in this report. A sample of this size would be large enough to provide measurement data disaggregated by substate regions and major population subgroups.

Role of the State Government:

A state government agency would provide financial support for and supervise the design of the survey and analysis of data. A survey firm probably should be given a contract to conduct the survey. Questions could be included regarding several aspects of the performance of several state agencies.[a]

Economic Development Measures Covered:

The survey would provide data for Measures 1, 2, 3, 4, 5, 6, 7, and 11 listed in Exhibit 1.

Timing of Data Collection and Reporting:

Survey data could be collected and reported according to the following schedule, assuming that the supervisory state agency, questionnaire, and sample had already been selected:

Interviewing	1st calendar month
Coding and tabulation	2nd and 3rd calendar months
Preparation of report	4th calendar month.

Cost and Staff Time Requirements:

Based on similar surveys in the states of Wisconsin and North Carolina, surveys of 1,500 to 2,000 households would cost a minimum of $25,000 to $40,000 annually, depending on interview method and the effort made to contact non-respondents. This sum includes costs of pretesting an already developed questionnaire, sample selection, and coding and tabulation of results. If several state agencies participated, the cost to each agency could be reduced substantially. In the early years of the survey, state agencies would have to devote considerable effort to developing the questionnaire's contents and format. In later years staff time requirements for these purposes would be small.

Feasibility:

The states of North Carolina and Wisconsin conducted surveys using questionnaires similar to Appendix A in 1976. Both surveys covered a wide range of services, including social services, health, and transportation as well as economic development. These tests suggest that such a survey is feasible and could be undertaken at reasonable cost to a state government. Further validity and reliability testing of questions on the survey is highly desirable, however.

[a]Other reports in this series recommend the use of a statewide survey for gathering data on state mental and physical health services, transportation services, and social services.

biases if response rates are low.[1] These methods vary in their cost per interview. The problems raised by each method also vary:

Response Rate

Mail surveys tend to have a lower initial response rate than other methods, even though the total number of responses is generally much higher. A mail survey can be inexpensively mailed to a very large number of potential respondents. Unlike mail surveys, telephone and in-person surveys must be adapted to hours of the day when respondents are likely to be at home. Telephone contacts are affected by unlisted telephone numbers, but random digit dialing techniques have reduced this problem considerably. A more important problem with telephone interviewing is that some citizens may not have phones. (In North Carolina, for example, 15 percent of the residents do not have telephones.) All methods are affected by the residential mobility of potential respondents.

Duration of the Interview

The length and complexity of mail questionnaires must be minimized to avoid reducing response rates. Telephone and in-person interviews are not as sensitive to length and complexity; interviews of thirty minutes to an hour have been used successfully. In-person interviews, unlike telephone calls, can make use of visual aids, but it has become increasingly difficult to obtain in-person contacts, particularly in areas with crime problems.

Confidentiality

Certain "sensitive" or "personal" questions may cause the respondent to refuse to respond or to terminate the interview. The respondent's sense of privacy may also affect the honesty of the response. Income-related questions are probably most vulnerable to these problems, although similar questions do not seem to be causing major difficulties in other surveys.[2] Where there is personal contact, however, such problems may be alleviated by rapport between interviewer and respondent.

The cost of a survey depends, of course, on the cost per contact and the size of the sample to be contacted. Using standard statistical procedures, North Carolina found that to estimate percentages to plus or minus five percentage points at an 80 percent confidence level, a minimum of about 164 responses would be needed. To be able to analyze survey results by eight subcategories

1. Joseph R. Hochstim, "A Critical Comparison of Three Strategies of Collecting Data from Households," Journal of American Statistical Association (September 1967), pp. 982-83.

2. For example, similar questions are currently being used in the monthly Current Population Survey (CPS) conducted by the Census Bureau, the Continuous Longitudinal Manpower Survey (CLMS) conducted by the U.S. Department of Labor, and the Detroit Citizen Survey conducted by the Planning Department of the City of Detroit.

(e.g., by race and four substate regions) with the above precision, a sample of about 1,400 would be needed. Sixteen subcategories would require a sample of about 2,700.

In addition, for in-person interviews, travel costs can become considerable, especially for those in the sample from rural areas.

Exhibit 3 shows cost estimates for sample sizes of 1,400 and 2,700 by mail, telephone, and in-person interview. These estimates cover (a) pretesting of the questionnaire, (b) conducting the interviews, (c) coding and keypunching the data, and (d) making a few basic tabulations of survey results. The estimates do not include (a) initial development of the questionnaire, (b) development of the population list from which a sample could be drawn, or (c) analysis of the survey results.

Estimates for in-person interviews were based on a rough projection of about $50 per positive contact. The cost of the telephone survey reflects a WATS line cost of $2.30 per interview. Telephone costs are shown both for an in-house survey (telephone costs only) and for a survey conducted by nongovernment employees (telephone and personnel costs). The mail estimates show out-of-pocket costs only and are based on previous state experience.

As shown in Exhibit 3, out-of-pocket costs for a sample of 1,400 range all the way from $5,600 for a short mail survey to $79,000 for a long in-person survey. These estimates suggest that the average marginal cost of increasing the length of the survey is $187 per minute for 1,400 persons and $3,600 per minute for 2,700 persons.

Costs were also estimated for three options which combine the different methods in order to benefit from the advantages of each. They are shown in Exhibit 4.

EXHIBIT 3

COSTS OF VARIOUS CITIZEN SURVEY METHODS[a]

Interview Length	Sample Size	Contracted In-Person Survey	Contracted Telephone Survey	In-House Telephone Survey	In-House Mail Survey
Short (15 min.)	1400	$ 74,200	$21,000	$ 8,400	$ 5,600
	2700	143,100	40,500	16,200	10,800
Medium (30 min.)	1400	77,000	23,800	11,200	7,000
	2700	148,500	45,900	21,600	13,500
Long (45 min.)	1400	79,800	26,600	14,000	12,600
	2700	153,900	51,300	27,000	24,300

[a]Data for this exhibit were provided by the North Carolina Department of Administration and based in part on estimates from private survey organizations. See also North Carolina, Division of State Budget and Management, How the Survey Was Conducted and What it Cost.

EXHIBIT 4

COSTS OF VARIOUS COMBINATIONS OF MAIL, TELEPHONE, AND IN-PERSON
SURVEYS FOR A MEDIUM-LENGTH (THIRTY-MINUTE) INSTRUMENT

	N=1,400	N=2,700
Option 1[a]		
Contracted Telephone (80%)	$19,040	$36,720
Contracted In-Person (20%)	15,400	29,700
	34,440	66,420
Option 2[b]		
In-House Mail (40%)	2,800	5,400
Contracted Telephone (40%)	9,520	18,360
Contracted In-Person (20%)	15,400	29,700
	$27,720	$53,460
Option 3[c]		
Contracted Telephone (60%)	14,280	27,540
Contracted In-Person (40%)		
Reachable by Phone (20%)	15,400	29,700
Not Reachable by Phone (20%)	15,400	29,700
	$45,080	$86,940

[a]Option 1: A contracted survey; primarily by telephone (80 percent), with in-person interview of those who cannot be contacted by telephone.

[b]Option 2: An in-house mail survey; assumes a 40 percent mail return, followed by contracted telephone and in-person surveys of nonrespondents. Because of the extra time needed to send second questionnaires to persons who do not respond by mail the first time, this option can take two months longer than Option 1.

[c]Option 3: Similar to Option 1, except that some of the respondents reachable by telephone are interviewed in person to determine whether responses from persons with and without telephones will differ. This option anticipates that 60 percent of the interviews will be conducted by telephone and 40 percent in person.

We do not recommend that a mail survey be conducted without extensive follow-up of nonrespondents. Otherwise the nonresponse bias will probably be too great and will not provide sufficiently credible results.

State household surveys were sponsored by the states of North Carolina and Wisconsin in 1976. These surveys covered economic development and other state program areas. In both cases, a professional survey organization was retained for pretesting, interviewing, coding and preparation of basic data, and for providing basic tabulations but no extensive analysis. The cost of these outside services in each of the two states was about $25,000. The North Carolina survey contacted about 1,400 households for telephone interviewing, with some in-person follow-up interviews for households that could not be reached by telephone. The Wisconsin survey contacted about 2,000 households by telephone. Therefore, the out-of-pocket costs were approximately $18 and $12.50 per household contacted, for North Carolina and Wisconsin, respectively.

In addition, North Carolina's Division of State Budget and Management estimated that the North Carolina survey incurred approximately $15,000 in additional costs for various set-up and analysis tasks, for a total cost of about $40,000.[1] This brought North Carolina total costs to about $29 per interview.

It was also estimated by North Carolina that about 78 percent of the total cost, or about $30,000, would be required to conduct approximately the same survey in subsequent years.[2]

Throughout this chapter reference has been made to an annual survey. Some states may wish to consider less frequent surveys, perhaps once every two years, since some measures may be fairly stable from one year to the next. If the survey were conducted less frequently, the state (for the same total cost) could increase the number of households sampled and thus reduce the variation in results due to sample size (in other words, smaller percentage changes in employment and income measures would have greater statistical significance).

Another option is for a state to conduct an annual survey to obtain data on those measures most likely to change from one year to the next (such an approach would probably focus on Measures 2 and 3) and obtain data for the other measures less frequently (perhaps every two years). However, the set-up costs are sufficiently large that the cost savings are likely to be small.

Whatever survey method a state chooses, good estimates of the employment and income measures specifically recommended in this report can only be obtained if low-income households are adequately represented. For example, if the survey were conducted by telephone, it is likely that low-income groups would be those with the lowest proportion of telephones. Although the overall rate of telephone subscription in North Carolina, for example, was 85 percent in 1975, the percentage was probably lower among low-income families. In the Wisconsin telephone

---

1. North Carolina, Division of State Budget and Management, How the Survey Was Conducted and What it Cost, p. 32.

2. Ibid.

survey, the Milwaukee area was intentionally oversampled, because the area was expected to contain most of the low-income (and minority) households in the state who otherwise would likely have not been sufficiently represented in the sample. Survey results were subsequently weighted in an attempt to alleviate this problem somewhat. In North Carolina, the sampling frame was selected from lists of persons filing income tax returns and Medicaid recipients to try to avoid underrepresentation of low-income households.

There is another sampling question which concerns the use of data collected in a survey of a random sample of state households to estimate outcome measures related to the status of the state's individuals rather than its households. In this chapter, we discuss the potential use of a household survey for four such measures: Measures 1 and 2 on the rate and duration of adult unemployment; Measure 4 on wage sufficiency for employed adults; and Measure 5 on job quality for employed adults (respondents only). In order to provide accurate estimates of these measures for a state's citizens, the sample of all adults (or in the case of Measure 4, the sample of respondents only) in the random sample of state households needs to approximate a random sample of state adults. We do not currently know the probable degree of similarity between these samples. Further study of this question is needed, using actual experience of states undertaking household surveys.

A Survey Instrument

An illustrative set of questions for a state household survey to collect data for the employment and income measures is shown in Appendix A. Measures pertinent to the individual questions are indicated in the left hand margin. These measures and questions have been discussed in the previous sections.

In adapting this or other survey instruments for its own use, a state should be careful not to omit any items which would be needed to calculate measures they want. In any case, the questionnaire decided on should be carefully pretested to assure that the wording is clear and appropriate for the state's own conditions and uses. As was indicated in the earlier sections of this chapter on individual outcome measures, there are potential problems with a single household respondent recalling information for the previous twelve months, and also providing answers regarding employment and earnings status of all adult household members. Additional state experience with the survey will be required to test the magnitude of these problems, if they occur, and to develop improved procedures to deal with them.

Presenting and Interpreting Survey Results

A state should look for variations in the survey responses for major population subgroups and substate regions. Exhibits 5 and 6 illustrate formats for highlighting such variations. Percentage responses are probably preferable to the actual number of those who responded to each response category, since they facilitate comparisons by household groupings. (The size and distribution of the sample surveyed should be made available to the users as illustrated in Exhibits 5 and 6.)

After survey data have been collected for more than one year, formats can be used to show trends, as in Exhibit 6.

EXHIBIT 5

ILLUSTRATIVE DISPLAY OF DATA: DEMOGRAPHIC GROUPINGS[a]

Grouping of Households	Number of Households	Percent of Respondents Rating Their Household Standard of Living During the Past Twelve Months as:			
		Excellent	Good	Fair	Poor
All Households	(1,400)	10	40	40	10
Households Whose Respondent Was:					
White Male	(250)	12	43	38	7
White Female	(650)	11	50	35	4
Nonwhite Male	(200)	6	21	55	18
Nonwhite Female	(300)	4	32	49	15
Households Whose Respondent Was:					
18-34	(500)	12	35	40	13
35-49	(350)	13	45	34	8
50-64	(350)	8	55	30	7
65 or Over	(200)	7	30	49	14
Households Whose Income Was:					
Under $5,000	(200)	0	0	60	40
$5,000-$9,999	(400)	0	21	59	20
$10,000-$14,999	(400)	0	51	49	0
$15,000-$19,999	(200)	24	66	10	0
$20,000 or More	(200)	30	70	0	0
Households by Substate Region:					
Central	(250)	16	38	39	7
Northeast	(450)	11	37	42	10
Northwest	(200)	4	25	51	20
Southeast	(350)	3	50	32	15
Southwest	(150)	13	46	34	7

[a]The numbers shown in this table are hypothetical.

EXHIBIT 6

ILLUSTRATIVE DISPLAY OF DATA: REGIONAL GROUPINGS[a]

	Percent of State Households with No Person Employed, and at Least One Person Looking for Work, for at Least Two Months in the Year Preceding the Household Survey in:		
	1977	1978	1979
Total State	5	6	4
Central Region	2	3	3
Northeast Region	5	5	4
Northwest Region	10	11	10
Southeast Region	7	5	4
Southwest Region	3	4	3
(Number of State Households)	(1,400)	(1,415)	(1,384)

[a]The numbers shown in this table are hypothetical.

Exhibits 5 and 6 illustrate different disaggregations of interest to state governments. Exhibit 5 shows breakdowns by major demographic groupings. Exhibit 6 shows measures for substate regions.

It will be important for the state to identify "key" findings so that the large body of data generated by the measurement procedures can be summarized for officials using the data. General guidelines for identifying three types of key findings are described below.[1]

Key Findings on Statewide Economic Conditions: Measures that suggest that economic conditions for the state as a whole are significantly better or worse than was "expected" or than state officials consider "desirable." Several sources might be used to compare measures based on survey results with what was

---

1. The sample's general representativeness of the state's households should be checked prior to analysis of survey results and selection of likely findings. The composition of the statewide sample should be compared with available statistics (such as data from the most recent decennial census) on all population subgroups and substate regions for which employment and income measures are being developed.

"expected" or "desired." The latter can be derived from official statements of state policy or targets set for economic development activities, measures of the same economic conditions calculated from other data sources, the results of similar household surveys in other places, and the results of earlier or similar surveys in the same state.[1]

Key Findings on Trends Over Time: Measures that suggest that a significant change in the state's (or a substate area's or a population subgroup's) employment or economic situation has taken place over time (after the survey has been conducted for more than one year). Economic development is a long-term process occurring over a period of many years. Therefore, relatively small numerical changes may be important if statistical tests indicate they are not likely to be due to chance (chance here being associated with "luck-of-the-draw" in selecting the sample of households to be surveyed in each year).[2] For example, a rise of a few points in the percentage of state households experiencing unemployment of four weeks or more may be of concern to state officials.

Key Findings on Differences Among Substate Areas or Population Subgroups: Measures that indicate that one or more substate regions or population subgroups are significantly different from the same measure(s) for the state as a whole. For many measures (such as household income), differences among substate regions or population subgroups will probably be greater than changes for the state as a whole over time. Again, tests of statistical significance will be needed to eliminate differences due to chance rather than changes in economic conditions. The smaller sample sizes for substate areas and population subgroups will mean that larger numerical differences will be required for statistical significance. As was the case with time trends, however, relatively small numerical differences may be of concern to state (and local) officials. For example, a substate region where 10 percent of the households had no person employed and at least one person looking for work or wanting to work but feeling that it was futile to look for work for at least one month in the preceding year may offer a key finding if the statewide household unemployment rate is 5 percent and the difference is not due to chance.

Interpretation and Validation. Once a key finding has been selected, its meaning must be interpreted carefully and cautiously. As noted in the summary of this report, most jobs and incomes are influenced by forces beyond the control of a state's economic development program.

We recommend that a person with training in regional economic analysis and familiarity with recent national and state economic trends participate in the

---

1. Survey findings which serve as the basis for a key finding should be checked for validity or reliability problems (such as those caused by a high nonresponse rate). If any questions arise, the finding should either be appropriately qualified or not presented as a key finding because of the problems noted. This applies to the findings discussed throughout this chapter.

2. For more specific procedures and tables to be used in assessing the statistical significance of particular differences or changes, a statistics textbook should be consulted. In many cases, a chi square test should be appropriate and relatively easy to calculate. An 80 percent level of confidence is probably sufficient for most of the uses to which citizen survey data are likely to be put.

analysis of results from the economic development portions of a state household survey.

Coordinating the Survey and Its Uses

The use of a statewide household survey to collect data for estimating employment and income measures, particularly for substate regions and population subgroups, involves a new data collection and processing procedure. The state should be alert to any difficulties in obtaining interviews from those in the sample and should identify those survey questions which appear to confuse respondents, those which appear to cause difficulty in recalling information, those which might cause respondents to answer inaccurately, and those which respondents refuse to answer.

Any problems identified in initial surveys will require attention in subsequent surveys. However, it will also be important to try to keep survey procedures and questions as similar as possible from one year to the next so that valid year-to-year comparisons can be made.

We estimate that an initial survey (including development of the questionnaire) will take approximately six to eight months. Surveys in subsequent years will probably take less time, perhaps three to four months. These estimates are based on the 1976 experiences of North Carolina and Wisconsin. Their surveys included some of the economic development questions recommended in this chapter as well as questions in other program areas (such as health and social services).

The North Carolina survey included questions for use in monitoring the outcomes of economic development and health programs, and was coordinated by the Division of State Budget and Management (DSBM) in the North Carolina Department of Administration.

A draft questionnaire and a random sample of about 1,600 households were provided to a private survey research agency which had obtained a state contract to undertake the survey in response to a request for proposals. This agency pretested the questionnaire, made some minor changes in it in consultation with DSBM, conducted the interviews, and provided survey data and a few basic tabulations to DSBM.

DSBM prepared more extensive tabulations of survey results and wrote a draft report on the survey's results. This draft report, completed in January 1977, included guidelines (such as confidence intervals and information on the validity of particular measures surveyed) for interpreting the results.

The Wisconsin survey included questions for use in monitoring the outcomes of economic development, social service, health, and transportation programs. The survey was coordinated by the Wisconsin Department of Administration (DoA).

A draft questionnaire was provided to the survey research laboratory of the state university which contracted to undertake the survey. The laboratory pretested the questionnaire, made some minor changes in it in consultation with DoA, conducted the interviews, and provided survey data to DoA. It also provided DoA with a computer printout on the statewide frequencies of responses for each survey question, but did no further tabulation of survey results.

In both North Carolina and Wisconsin, several months of state government staff time were spent in designing procedures which had not been tried by any other state (in particular, the development of the questionnaires). For the first survey in another state, time will be required to develop a questionnaire which fits the interests of the state agencies involved. In subsequent years less state government staff time will be required. The survey contract can be updated, and data processing, analysis, and report writing will become more routine.

Chapter 2

OUTCOME MEASURES FOR JOB CREATION
THROUGH INDUSTRIAL DEVELOPMENT

Industrial development commonly consists of "activities designed to achieve economic growth and development primarily through attracting new industries to the region or aiding in the expansion of existing industry . . . ."[1]

State industrial development agencies offer several services to new or expanding industrial firms. These services include analyses of labor, raw material, and product markets, and other data related to possible industrial sites; arranging for financial and other types of incentives; and assistance in obtaining permits and licenses from local, state, and federal agencies. Industrial development agencies also advise state and local governments on ways to improve their jurisdictions' industrial potential.

Throughout this chapter the term "industrial firm" is used in the broadest sense to include all types of manufacturing, processing, and other employment-producing operations. The significant issues are (1) whether the firms contacted decided to locate or expand within the state and (2) whether the state government, and particularly its state industrial development programs, played a role in the firms' decisions. The outcome monitoring procedures described here attempt to provide estimates on both issues, but are particularly directed at providing information on the second issue.

Key Measurement Issues

Exhibit 7 lists suggested outcome measures and associated data collection procedures for annual monitoring of state industrial development programs. These measures reflect two types of outcomes: (1) the impact of new or expanded firms, and (2) the perceptions of industrial firms regarding the quality of the state industrial development services which they received.

The objective of state industrial development programs is to increase employment opportunities and earnings by attracting new firms to the state and helping resident firms to expand. These state agencies also attempt to avoid

---

1. Alfred W. Swinyard, et al., State Economic Development (Ann Arbor: Bureau of Business Research, University of Michigan, 1967), p. 7.

EXHIBIT 7

SUGGESTED OUTCOME MEASURES FOR INDUSTRIAL DEVELOPMENT

Objective	Suggested Measure	Data Collection or Estimation Procedures
Increase or maintain employment	1a. Number of jobs in new or expanded industrial firms which had contact with state industrial development agencies	Estimates by industrial firms (before location or expansion), independent state projections, firm data (after location or expansion)
	1b. Number of jobs in new or expanded industrial firms which indicated that their decision to locate or expand in the state was significantly influenced by assistance provided by state industrial development agencies or other types of direct state assistance	State-sponsored survey of industrial clients (plus employment estimates, as in 1a)
Avoid job losses	2. Number of industrial jobs lost due to (a) exit from the state or (b) permanent reductions in the scale of production of resident firms	Local employment security offices, contact with industrial firms or independent state estimates
Increase income	3a. Dollar amount of wages and salaries from jobs in new or expanded industrial firms which had contact with state industrial development agencies	Estimates by industrial firms (before location or expansion), independent state projections, firm data (after location or expansion)
	3b. Dollar amount of wages and salaries from jobs in industrial firms which indicated that their decision to locate or expand in the state was significantly influenced by assistance provided by state industrial development agencies or other types of direct state assistance	State-sponsored survey of industrial clients (plus wage estimates, as in 3a)
Attract industries	4a. Number of industrial firms which located or expanded in the state after contact with state industrial development agencies	Records of state industrial development agencies

EXHIBIT 7 (CONT'D)

Objective	Suggested Measure	Data Collection or Estimation Procedures
Attract industries (cont'd)	4b. Number of industrial firms which indicated that their decision to locate or expand in the state was significantly influenced by assistance provided by state industrial development agencies or other types of direct state assistance	State-sponsored survey of industrial clients
	5. Number and percent of former industrial prospects that cited various factors that can be influenced by the state as reasons for their decision not to locate, expand, or remain in the state	State-sponsored survey of industrial clients
Minimize user dissatisfaction with state assistance	6. Percent of industrial firms which had contact with state industrial development agencies and rated the assistance which they received as "fair" or "poor"	State-sponsored survey of industrial clients
Minimize detrimental impacts	7. Number and percent of the new firms assisted by the state which significantly degraded the environment	Ratings of new firms

closures and reductions in the scale of company operations. Measures 1, 3, and 4 deal with the outcomes of state assistance to new and expanding firms: Measure 2 deals with the outcome of attempts to prevent reductions or closures.

Most states compile data on new employment due to the decisions of industrial firms to locate or expand their operations within the state. These data usually consist of estimates made by the firms prior to the start of operations. These estimated levels of employment, however, often are not reached, due to changes in a firm's plans as the start of operations approaches. If a state intends to use employment projections as outcome measures, such data should be treated as mere estimates and should be compared with actual employment levels once full plant operation is reached. For the sake of accuracy it is preferable to utilize actual employment and earnings data for outcome measures.

Measuring the outcome of state industrial development activities is complicated by the difficulty of showing a causal relationship between industrial decisions and state efforts. This problem has two major facets.

First, many factors which are beyond state control influence firms' location and expansion decisions. These factors include availability of land, facilities, and raw materials; closeness of markets; labor quality and supply; and fuel and transportation costs. To alleviate this, at least partially, Measures 1, 3, and 4 are each stated in two forms. One form (the "a" form of the measure) states the number of positive outcomes (e.g., number of new firms in the state which had contact with the state), and does not attempt to attribute the outcomes to program efforts. The second form (the "b" form) begins with the number of positive outcomes and, by using follow-up surveys of industrial clients (discussed below) to assess the significance of state efforts, counts only those outcomes in which the state was identified by the client as having had a "significant influence." The validity of this judgment expressed by the client is not clear, but the attempt to link outcome data to state efforts seems desirable.

The second problem in relating outcomes to state efforts is that a firm's decision may be influenced by various state agencies (e.g., transportation, education) and state laws (e.g., those pertaining to taxes, employment, financial incentives, the environment). Data on Measure 5 (number of former prospects that cited various factors that can be influenced by the state as reasons for not locating in the state) may provide some general indication of the influence of state agencies and laws on the achievement of state industrial development goals--at least of negative aspects.

The relative importance of the factors affecting a firm's decision can only be determined by in-depth analyses that may require some form of controlled experimentation. Such analyses are costly and can rarely be conducted by state government. The outcome measures presented here are weak in their ability to attribute industrial decisions to the efforts of the state industrial development offices only. They are at best a first step toward better monitoring tools, offered on the presumption that states are interested in monitoring the outcomes of state industrial development efforts even if information on immediate causal factors is limited.

Measures of new employment, earnings, and industrial firms should be subdivided, wherever appropriate, to monitor progress toward special state development subobjectives as well as for the state as a whole. For example, a development objective might be to channel growth into certain under-developed regions of the state. This objective could be monitored by tabulating Measure 1 (number of new jobs in firms which had contact with the state) by substate region to indicate the extent to which new jobs were being created in target areas. Another example would be to disaggregate new jobs created according to wage level, if improving the average wage level in the state (or substate area) were a major development objective.

The principal new data collection procedure recommended here is a survey of industrial firms which have been assisted by the state. It is suggested for several purposes:

(a) To estimate the significance of state assistance in attracting new employment, earnings, and industrial firms (for Measures 1b, 3b, and 4b);

(b) To indicate which factors that might have been affected by the state may have influenced decisions not to locate, expand, or remain in the state (for Measure 5); and

(c) To measure industrial clients' perceptions of the quality of various aspects of state services, such as timeliness, relevance, and overall helpfulness (for Measure 6).[1]

The last section of this chapter contains a brief description of the proposed survey procedures. Appendix B contains an illustrative set of survey questions.

In addition to the measures referred to above, the possible detrimental effects of industrial development should also be monitored. These include the impacts of new or expanded facilities on air, water, and noise pollution levels, traffic congestion, and use of energy resources. Some limited monitoring of these factors can be achieved by grouping data on new firms into three-to-five categories based on their potential detrimental effects (e.g., categories based on percent of likely compliance with pollutant discharge standards). Other than this limited form of monitoring, it is suggested that detrimental effects be examined by special studies which periodically consider all firm location or expansion decisions as a group, or review possible detrimental effects in detail as individual decisions are announced.

---

1. For most measures there is likely to be a time lag between state efforts and results. A firm's decision to locate in the state may be announced several years after the state provided its assistance. However, for Measure 6, it is appropriate to obtain the information on the quality of state services as perceived by users (e.g., industrial prospects and local development groups) prior to the firm's decision.

Individual Outcome Measures of Industrial Development Activities

1a. Number of jobs in new or expanded industrial firms which had
contact with state industrial development agencies.

1b. Number of jobs in new or expanded industrial firms which
indicated their decision to locate or expand in the state was
significantly influenced by assistance provided by state
industrial development agencies or other types of direct state
assistance.

3a. Dollar amount of wages and salaries from jobs in new or expanded
industrial firms which had contact with state industrial development agencies.

3b. Dollar amount of wages and salaries from jobs in industrial
firms which indicated that their decision to locate or expand
in the state was significantly influenced by assistance provided by state industrial development agencies or other types
of direct state assistance.

4a. Number of industrial firms which located or expanded in the state
after contact with state industrial development agencies.

4b. Number of industrial firms which indicated that their decision
to locate or expand in the state was significantly influenced by
assistance provided by state industrial development agencies or
other types of direct state assistance.[1]

These measures attempt to assess the impact of industrial development
efforts on three key variables: employment, income, and number of industrial
firms in the state.

We have included both employment and income here because they can have
different economic impacts. High-wage jobs are preferable to low-wage jobs,
but high-wage jobs for a few may not be as desirable as lower-wage jobs for
many.

Although it is the easiest data to obtain, the "number of firms making
affirmative decisions" should not be used as the only outcome measure because
firms vary greatly in the magnitude of their effects on employment and income.

---

1. A variation of this measure, the percentage of industrial firms which
had contact with state industrial development agencies and which located or expanded
in the state, was considered but was not included because it might discourage
state industrial recruiters from pursuing "longshot" industrial prospects which
would lower the percentage.

These measures include only the impacts of firms which had contact with the state development agency pertaining to a possible location or expansion of industrial operations. The decisions of firms that located or expanded in the state without utilizing state industrial development services are not included, since they probably are not attributable to the activities of state industrial development agencies.

Data Collection Procedures

Gathering Data on Employment and Earnings

Most states gather data on the number of jobs and earnings from new and expanded firms and that data could be used for Measures 1a, 3a, and 4a. These data are collected by mail and personal contacts with firms, most often prior to the firms' hiring of new employees.

Exhibit 8 is the form currently used by North Carolina to gather employment and earnings data from new or expanded firms. This form is mailed to firms by the industrial development agency soon after the firm announces its decision to locate or expand in the state. Nonrespondents are contacted by telephone. Agency staff members report that very few businesses have refused to provide employment and earnings data. North Carolina's experience is consistent with the findings from a survey of new firms in seventeen southeastern states which found that only 10 percent of the firms were either unwilling or unable to provide data on the number of jobs.[1] This survey, however, encountered a great problem in gathering wage data from businesses; 25 percent were willing but unable to provide information on payrolls for new positions, and 5 percent were unable to make estimates of future payrolls.

Measures 1a, 3a, and 4a should probably exclude the impacts of firms which had only trivial contact with the state agency. Developing a standardized definition of a "nontrivial contact" could be difficult. It is unlikely that a satisfactory definition would be based on either the number of contacts or on the point in the firm's decision-making process at which the state provided assistance.[2] A stringent standard is probably not possible. Instead, contacts included in the measure should probably include all but those which were "courtesy calls" by firm or state representatives.

Most states gather data on new or increased employment and earnings immediately after announcement of the firm's location or expansion decision. This may result in inaccuracies because economic conditions and other factors may cause the firm to alter the scale of production from what it originally anticipated. As a first step in a 1963 study of new industries, researchers

1. William R. Thomas, "Toward Criteria for Evaluating the Effectiveness of Organized Industrial Development Effort," AIDC Journal (October 1973), p. 68.

2. Assistance provided after the firm announces its locational decision may be crucial in insuring a positive outcome because at this point the state can facilitate relationships between the firm and federal, state, and local agencies.

EXHIBIT 8

ILLUSTRATIVE QUESTIONNAIRE FOR GATHERING INDUSTRIAL EMPLOYMENT AND EARNINGS OUTCOME DATA[a]

CONFIDENTIAL

ECONOMIC GROWTH RECORD SURVEY

Company Name _____
Mailing Address _____
Town _____ Zip _____
County _____
Parent Company _____
Address _____

Type of Investment (Check One)
___ Expansion (At Existing Location)
___ New Facility
Street Address _____
Town _____
County _____
Local Manager _____
Title _____
Start-Up Date _____

Type of Business Activity
If Manufacturing, List Product(s) _____
If Non-Manufacturing, Describe Type of Activity(s) _____

Planned Investment   (Check One)

Land   ___ Leased
Acres _____   ___ Purchased

Buildings   ___ Leased
Square Feet _____   ___ Purchased   Cost _____
   ___ Constructed

Other Improvements   ___ Leased
   ___ Purchased   Cost _____
   ___ Constructed

Equipment   ___ Leased   Cost _____
   ___ Previously Owned
   ___ Purchased   Value _____

New or Additional Employment   Anticipated Payroll
to be Generated by This Investment
Hourly Wage Earners _____   Average Hourly Wage _____
Salaried Employees _____   Average Monthly Salary _____

Ultimate Total
Employment Anticipated
At This Site _____

Return to: Miss Virginia Satterfield
Division of Economic Development
N.C. Dept. of Nat. & Econ. Resources
P.O. Box 27687
Raleigh, North Carolina 27611   Phone: (919) 829-5816

Dear North Carolina Businessman:

The Division of Economic Development continually seeks to record and report business investments and the resulting jobs created in activities considered generators of economic growth. Aggregate figures are announced quarterly and annually by the Governor or the Secretary of our Department of Natural and Economic Resources. They are important indicators of North Carolina's economic progress as related to the effectiveness of development programs; current business trends; the attractiveness of North Carolina to investors; and, in general, the overall health of our economy.

We solicit your assistance in securing the information requested on the attached survey form. Our records are kept strictly confidential, with the data used only for cumulative State and regional totals. Under no circumstances are individual plant data revealed.

Thank you for your time and efforts in completing the form and returning it to us. An expeditious reply would be greatly appreciated.

Sincerely yours,

Robert E. Leak

[a] SOURCE: State of North Carolina, Department of Natural and Economic Resources, Division of Economic Development.

compiled a list of firms which between January 1953 and the spring of 1958 had announced their intention to locate in North Carolina. Only 193 of the approximately 400 firms (48 percent) on this list existed by 1958-1960 because, according to the study, ". . . apparently--(1) a number of 'proposed' new plants had never gone into production; (2) many new firms had gone out of business shortly after starting up; (3) others were not really 'new' in terms of the sample definition, or not actually engaged in the manufacture of a product."[1] This indicates that the initial information on employment and income provided by new firms is likely to provide an incorrect picture of what actually happens.

One method for reducing this probable error is to apply the U.S. Economic Development Administration's (EDA) "risk factors" to industrial employment projections. Examples of EDA risk factors are as follows:

(a) 100 percent of specified impact is credited if plant or expansion is completed and hiring has begun at the time the projections are made.

(b) 75 percent of specified impact is credited if plant or expansion is completed but hiring has not yet begun.

(c) 50 percent of specified impact is credited if plant or expansion is under construction and completion is expected within one year.

(d) 25 percent of specified impact is credited if plant or expansion is not under construction but completion is expected within one year.

(e) No impact is credited if none of the above apply.[2]

The above risk factors might be used or the state might develop its own risk factors, based on comparisons of past employment projections with employment and earnings levels later achieved at full production.

This approach would produce timely estimates for monitoring the outcomes of state industrial recruitment efforts, but it is probably preferable to base outcome measurements on actual employment and earnings data gathered after start-up.

The North Carolina industrial development agency administers the questionnaire in Exhibit 8 after a firm's location or expansion announcement and also after start-up. The two sets of data are compared to determine the degree of change in plans. While delaying compilation of these data until after start-up provides the most accurate basis for measuring the

1. Ruth L. Mace, Industry and City Government (Chapel Hill, N.C.: Institute of Government, University of North Carolina, 1963), pp. ix-x.

2. U.S., Department of Commerce, Economic Development Administration, Developing Methodologies for Evaluating the Impact of EDA Programs (Washington, D.C., January 1972), p. 12

impact of new firms assisted by the state, these data may not be available for several years after the initial contacts with the firms, thus considerably reducing the data's usefulness.[1]

Several issues related to the definition of "job" arise in calculating these measures:

(a) Seasonal and part-time jobs. Seasonal and part-time jobs should be tabulated in a consistent fashion. One approach is to count such jobs in terms of their annual "full-time" equivalents. Another is to tabulate the number of full-time nonseasonal jobs separately from jobs which are seasonal or part-time. (This latter approach seems preferable because of the distinct nature of seasonal and part-time employment.)

(b) Construction employment. Many jobs are created by the construction of new or expanded facilities. It is difficult to estimate accurately the number of these jobs because many employers are involved in construction and a relatively high proportion of jobs are created by suppliers and subcontractors working off-site. Therefore, if such estimates are made, standardized procedures should be carefully followed (e.g., what classes or construction-related jobs are included) and the data should be stated separately from data on direct employment by the industrial firm.

(c) Indirect employment. New industrial activity also stimulates new jobs in the region due to "multiplier effects" on residential construction, services, and commercial activity. The magnitude of these effects varies according to the type of new industrial firm. The state may wish to experiment by making rough estimates of indirect employment, but precise calculation is probably beyond the scope of monitoring. These estimates, if attempted, should also be listed separately from direct employment.[2]

(d) In all of the above cases, some of the jobs created may be filled by persons from another state, especially if the site is near a state border or if the new firm is transferring a permanent facility from another state. The state may wish to make rough estimates of the number of such jobs to reflect more accurately the likely impact of the new activity on state unemployment.

Several issues also arise with regard to estimating increased income. For the sake of simplicity, it is probably advisable to base income measures on gross wages and salaries. This would exclude employer contributions to

---

1. It should be recognized that outcome measurements based on projections are not outcome measurements in the pure sense. Only measurements of what actually happened are, by definition, outcome measurements.

2. Thomas Muller, Economic Impacts of Land Development: Employment, Housing, and Property Values (Washington, D.C.: The Urban Institute, 1976); see pp. 15-35 for suggestions of simple methods for estimating indirect employment stimulated by new development activity.

social security, unemployment compensation, health and retirement, and other benefits which ultimately contribute to the economic well-being of the individual and the state. Such benefits, however, are very difficult to calculate. Gross wages and salaries include deductions for social security, state and federal taxes, and retirement and benefits even though these are not received in cash by the employee and do not immediately contribute to the economic well-being of the individual or the state.

Measures 1b, 3b, and 4b count only those firms whose decisions were "significantly influenced" by state assistance. Estimating the state's influence on a firm's decision is extremely difficult. A crude approximation can be attempted by means of a survey of former industrial clients after location or expansion decisions have been made. Appendix B contains an illustrative questionnaire for this survey. Responses to Question 4 of "very positive influence" or "somewhat positive influence" could be regarded as indicating that the state agency was a "significant influence" on the firm's decision.

Because it probably would not be possible to obtain responses to this questionnaire from all new firms, data on Measures 1b, 3b, and 4b would represent only the impacts of new and expanded firms which indicated in response to the survey that the state had a significant influence on their decision-making. Measures 1a, 3a, and 4a should be stated along with Measures 1b, 3b, and 4b for completeness.

The questionnaire in Appendix B should be administered shortly after a firm's decision to locate in the state has been announced. For a firm which was not assisted until after its location decision, such as a firm receiving state assistance only in obtaining operating permits, the questionnaire should be administered shortly after start-up.

For gathering outcome data, both surveys (Exhibit 8 and Appendix B) could be combined on the same form. This is not recommended, however, because of the frequently long period (perhaps several years) after a location or expansion decision has been made before accurate estimates on new or increased employment and earnings could be collected using the questionnaire in Exhibit 8.

There is also a need for more field experience with the questionnaire in Appendix B. The questionnaire in Exhibit 8 has obtained high response rates, probably due largely to the rapport between firms and state industrial representatives. The questions in Appendix B should not be administered by those in the agency whose work is in effect being assessed because this might result in biased (favorable) responses. In addition, the less traditional nature of the data collected by the form in Appendix B might reduce the rate of response to questions in Exhibit 8 if the two forms were combined.[1]

---

1. A further difference should be pointed out. The form in Exhibit 8 would be administered only to firms which have decided to locate or expand in the state. For Measures 5 and 6, the survey in Appendix B would be administered to all firms which had contact with the state, regardless of their final decision.

> 2. Number of industrial jobs lost due to (a) exit from the state or (b) permanent reductions in the scale of production of resident firms.

Many state industrial development agencies work with existing firms to avoid loss of jobs due to closures or permanent reductions in production. This measure is designed to monitor the outcome of these efforts.

Data Collection Procedures

Unfortunately, many plant closures and reductions in work force do not come to the attention of state industrial development officials. Local employment security agency offices appear to be more aware of such actions through their job placement functions and other services to the unemployed. Therefore, these offices may be able to provide fairly accurate data on this measure. It would be necessary for states to make special arrangements with local offices for systematic reporting of these data.

Because this measure's primary concern is closures and work force reductions which have a substantial effect on local unemployment, a state could set a minimum standard for reporting, such as "any closure or reduction in force involving more than twenty persons in a single year." Although this measure pertains to permanent or long-term changes, a subcategory of this measure might report reductions or closures of a temporary nature, but with a minimum duration (perhaps "more than four weeks").

> 5. Number and percent of former industrial prospects that cited various factors that can be influenced by the state as reasons for their decision not to locate, expand, or remain in the state.

Decisions on industrial location and scale of operation are complex. They are based on factors which are often very difficult to identify, and many of these factors are outside the purview of state industrial development officials. However, state policy can affect such factors as tax structure, availability of energy, natural resources, or raw materials, sewage treatment capacity, transportation facilities, labor force, and public improvements, and thereby influence industrial decisions. Furthermore, states also provide direct assistance to industrial prospects, ranging from advertising to financial incentives.

Information on the effects of factors that can be influenced by the state on the decisions of industrial prospects can provide the basis for changes in state policies. Determining the impact of factors beyond state government control may also provide insights which may be helpful in designing promotional campaigns and identifying firms on which to concentrate state promotional efforts.

The purpose of this measure is twofold: (a) to identify systematically those factors which influence industrial location decisions, with emphasis upon those factors which can be affected by state policies, and (b) by tabulating these factors annually, to help analyze long-term trends.

Data Collection Procedures

Data for this measure would be gathered by means of the follow-up survey, suggested above, of firms which had contact with state industrial development representatives. It is highly desirable to include firms which considered locating in the state but did not contact state representatives, but such firms are difficult to identify systematically in the recommended set of follow-up survey questions. The next section of this chapter outlines procedures for this survey. (Question 8 in Appendix B provides a means for grouping responses by whether firms did or did not decide to locate in the state.)

An initial data collection problem is to formulate a survey question which can obtain a response that can identify key influences among the many factors which affect a firm's locational decision. An approach which has been used in special studies is to list many possible factors in the questionnaire. The respondent is asked to indicate the importance of each factor on the firm's decision.[1] By including a large number of possibly influential factors there seems to be less likelihood of "ideological responses" by respondents than if the response were unguided. Question 4 in Appendix B illustrates this approach. approach.

Two other data collection problems are present with this measure: identification of an "appropriate respondent" and obtaining an "honest response." These problems are discussed in the next section, along with other issues related to the survey.

---

6. Percent of industrial firms which had contact with state industrial development agencies and rate the assistance which they received as "fair" or "poor."

The state provides industrial clients with a variety of services, including special studies (such as labor and product market analyses and site studies), site tours, and liaison services with governmental agencies. This measure calls for systematic ratings of the quality of these services by means of a survey of industrial prospects. Quality factors rated might include reliability, cooperativeness, promptness, and the relevance of the information provided.

Data Collection Procedures

Data for this measure would be collected as part of the same follow-up survey mentioned above and discussed further later. Questions 2 and 3 in Appendix B are designed to gather data on this measure.

Since this measure focuses on the quality of the state service, as distinct from the firm's locational decision, it is not essential that data collection be

---

1. Gerald J. Karaska and David F. Bramhall, eds., Locational Analysis for Manufacturing (Cambridge: Massachusetts Institute of Technology Press, 1969).

postponed until after the firm's decision. The questions could be administered shortly after key contacts with the firm (e.g., after a series of site visits). However, the most appropriate timing of these questions seems to be after the firm's decision, because at that time the firm would have an opinion of the entire state promotional effort.

> 7. Number and percent of the new firms assisted by the state which significantly degraded the environment.

Increasingly, state industrial development agencies are being held accountable for the environmental quality of industries attracted into the state. Measure 7 is intended to monitor how well the industrial development agency is helping to avoid the detrimental environmental effects of economic growth.

Data Collection Procedures

Measure 7 reports the number of firms which exceeded preselected levels of detrimental effects. A first step toward determining whether a specific firm exceeded these levels is to develop a standardized scale for measuring environmental effects. This scale would be used to rate new firms by one of two possible methods. One method would focus on one or two of the most significant pollutants and rate firms by whether they emitted more than the specified (maximum tolerable) levels of these pollutants.

Another method would be to use an overall rating scale that included several different types of environmental effects. This scale might assign a numerical value to each environmental effect (e.g., 0 = not detrimental and not helpful; +2 = somewhat helpful; and +4 = very helpful). This latter method would allow consideration of a broader variety of environmental effects than the first method.

Using the first method, Measure 7 would be the number and percent of all firms assisted by the state which exceeded maximum tolerable pollutant levels. Using the second method, Measure 7 would be the number and percent of industries which fell within a "detrimental" range on a numerical scale.

Estimates underlying Measure 7 would probably focus on air and water pollutants because techniques to measure these are better developed than techniques to measure other effects. Nevertheless, other effects (such as noise levels, traffic congestion, induced residential growth, and consumption of land with unique scenic, historical, or agricultural value) could also be given some consideration in a rating scale.

This measure applies only to new industries which had contact with the state's industrial development agency. In contrast, Measures 8, 9, and 10 in Chapter 1 considered the environmental effects of the whole range of existing industries.

Survey of Firms

Measures 1b, 3b, 4b, 5, and 6 obtain their data from a survey of firms which have been assisted by state representatives. Appendix B illustrates questions that might be included in such a survey. To the left of each question is the number of the measure to which it pertains. The questionnaire in Appendix B was adapted from a 1971 mail survey of 493 industrial firms which had been assisted by state industrial development agencies in the seventeen southeastern states.[1]

The questionnaire is designed to be administered to industrial prospects after they have made their location or expansion decision. To obtain earlier feedback, such a survey could be conducted prior to the firm's decision. However, responses prior to the firm's decision would not reflect later state contacts nor the firm's actual decision. The questionnaire also could be simplified by excluding all sections of Question 4 except those used for Measures 1b, 3b, and 4b.

A study of new North Carolina firms provided some clues regarding the willingness of industrial executives to complete surveys such as this.[2] This study involved an attempt to conduct personal and mail interviews of the executives of 193 plants. Of these, 161 were successfully interviewed, representing 71 percent of the new plants or 93 percent of total employment in plants in the sample. The lowest response rate was that of the thirty-eight plants with the smallest employment (one to twenty-nine employees). Among this group, twenty of the thirty-eight firms were contacted successfully, a response rate of approximately 55 percent. These small plants were contacted entirely by mail, with a single follow-up letter to nonrespondents, indicating either that small plants had a lower tendency to respond to letters or that in-person interviews were more successful in obtaining responses.

Interviews for the North Carolina study were conducted by private researchers. We do not know whether state governments would achieve higher or lower response rates. However, a similar set of in-person interviews was

---

1. William R. Thomas, State Industrial Development Organizations in the Southeast: An Evaluation of Performance by Industrial Executives (Atlanta: Georgia State University, 1971).
   For other survey questionnaires, see U.S., Economic Development Administration, Developing Methodologies. (These surveys are directed at industrial development organizations.)
   Employee and business survey forms have also been used by the EDA Growth Center Evaluation task force. See U.S., Department of Commerce, Economic Development Administration, Program Evaluation: Economic Development Administration Growth Center Strategy (Washington, D.C., February 1972).
   A more detailed questionnaire for use by local government officials is included in: Mace, Industry and City Government.

2. Mace, Industry and City Government.

conducted in the course of an evaluation by the City of San Diego, and no firms refused to provide requested information in that survey.[1]

The questionnaire included in Appendix B is worded for use by mail. In-person and particularly telephone interviews should be considered as alternatives, however, especially where more detailed information is desired.

Whether a survey such as this is feasible depends on the resolution of two major concerns:

First, identification of an "appropriate respondent." It is important to ensure that the respondent was sufficiently involved in the decision to provide a knowledgeable response. Thomas's approach seems useful here: request that the "person who acted as liaison between (the) firm and the (state development organization)" complete the questionnaire.[2] The problem of locating a knowledgeable respondent may be lessened somewhat if the questionnaire is mailed by the state directly to the firm's liaison person with whom state representatives dealt.

Second, obtaining an "honest" response. This concern has two dimensions:

(1) The respondent may provide favorable feedback out of a desire to maintain good relations with the state. One precaution that might be taken is to indicate clearly in the cover letter that the survey is part of an independent evaluation. Added assurance might be provided if an office which is organizationally separate from the industrial development department conducted the survey (e.g., the state planning office) with a cover letter stating that individual responses would not be revealed to the department involved.

(2) Question 4 may be vulnerable to "strategic" responses, where the respondent answers in a manner calculated to influence state policy rather than to reflect the reasons for a decision. To guard against this, a broad variety of factors are included in Question 4, including several categories of personal or nonbusiness reasons. Questions similar to this have been used in private studies, but their validity is still in question.

The list of questions in Appendix B is presented as an illustrative approach to regular monitoring of the quality of industrial development services. The questionnaire has not been tested, and the procedures involved in its administration require development and testing before it can be used with confidence in a monitoring system.

---

1. City of San Diego, Management Evaluation: Economic Development Corporation Evaluation, Comprehensive Management Planning Program, 76-514 (San Diego, 3 March 1976).

2. Thomas, Evaluation of Performance.

Chapter 3

OUTCOME MEASURES FOR JOB CREATION
THROUGH TOURISM PROMOTION

Tourism promotion is an economic development strategy often used to compensate for deficiencies in a state's industrial base or to stimulate economic growth. State government tourism promotion ranges from general advertising (e.g., newspapers, radio, and television or travel booths and shows) to more specific activities such as seeking to attract conventions and organizing travel packages. Most states also mail travel brochures to potential tourists at their request and operate information centers along major highways.

The state may also assist in the construction of facilities (e.g., public camp grounds, convention centers) or attempt to have them located where they will serve to attract travelers (e.g., a major hotel or convention facility or an amusement park). This chapter focuses on monitoring promotional efforts which seek to increase state employment and income through the attraction of larger numbers of tourists.

Key Measurement Issues

Exhibit 9 lists suggested outcome measures for tourism promotion and associated data collection procedures. This section summarizes the measurement approaches suggested in this chapter. The specific measures are discussed individually in the second section of this chapter.

Measures of Tourism-Related Employment and Income (Measures 1 and 2)

The magnitudes of additional employment and income generated by tourism are the key performance criteria for tourism promotion (Measures 1 and 2). The changes revealed by these measures, however, cannot be attributed solely to state efforts because:

(a) The number of tourists is greatly affected by factors beyond state control, such as private attractions and climate.

EXHIBIT 9

SUGGESTED OUTCOME MEASURES FOR TOURISM PROMOTION

Objective	Suggested Measure	Data Collection or Estimation Procedures
Increase employment	1. Estimated number of jobs directly related to tourism	Adaptation of state employment estimates
Increase income	2. Estimated dollar amount of tourist expenditures	Adaptation of state government tax records
Attract tourists	3a. Estimated number of tourists who visited the state from target tourism markets	Estimates based on counts of travelers
	3b. Estimated percent of potential tourists who visited the state from target tourism markets	Estimates based on counts of travelers and estimates of potential travel market
	4. Number of persons who visited the state as participants in tourism-related events sponsored or substantially assisted by the state government	Estimates of the number of participants in state-sponsored or state-assisted travel opportunities (e.g., travel packages, special events)
	5a. Number and percent of households that requested tourism assistance from the state that later visited the state	Follow-up survey of users of state government tourism services
	5b. Number and percent of households that requested tourism assistance from the state that indicated that they visited the state at least partly as a result of the assistance which they received	Follow-up survey of users of state government tourism services
	6. Number and percent of households that requested tourism assistance from the state that indicated that they have not yet visited the state for a reason which the state might have influenced	Follow-up survey of users of state government tourism services
Minimize user dissatisfaction with state assistance	7. Number and percent of households that requested tourism assistance from the state that rated the services which they received as "fair" or "poor"	Follow-up survey of users of state government tourism services

(b)   Tourism promotion achieves its objectives indirectly, by
        attracting tourists who in turn create employment and
        income by their spending. Therefore, the decisions of
        tourists and private businesses, after they are in the
        state, also greatly affect the level of tourism-related
        employment and earnings.

As a consequence, tourism-related employment and earnings in the state
as a whole are a weak measure of program-related outcomes. However, when
such data are tabulated by substate region they may provide more meaningful
indications of program-related outcomes.[1] This is because:

(a)   By comparing changes in annual outcome data for substate
        regions where there have been state efforts to promote
        tourism, information can be obtained as to whether changes
        in earning and income occurred subsequent to changes in
        promotional efforts.

(b)   It is also possible to determine whether tourism-related
        employment is occurring in regions of greatest need (such
        as those experiencing high unemployment).

(c)   The effects of privately sponsored events and promotions
        on outcome data can be more easily identified for particular
        substate regions.

For monitoring purposes it is also important that measurement data identify yearly changes in employment and earnings related to those types of
tourists which the state seeks to attract by its promotional efforts. We
suggest that Measures 1 and 2 focus on employment and earnings in a few narrowly defined types of business which are most likely to be affected by state
efforts (such as hotels and motels or commercial sports).

Measures of Outcomes for Tourism Advertising and Promotional Services (Measures 3a, 3b, 4, 5a, 5b, 6, and 7)

This chapter also includes measures of the outcomes of general advertising and assistance provided directly to potential tourists. Such promotional activities are directed at different but overlapping groups:

All potential tourists (Group A): This group is composed largely
of persons who might not consider travel to the state if it were
not for state promotion. The state attempts to stimulate this
group's interest by such means as general media advertisements,
press releases and travel columns, and organization of travel
packages, conventions, and special events.

_____

1. These regions are likely to be multi-county planning areas (for coordin-
ation with other economic development activities), although they might consist
of a single county or another type of tourism area in the state.

Potential tourists who receive state travel assistance directly
(Group B): This group has shown interest in the state by requesting
travel assistance, either at roadside information centers or through
the mail.

The measurement issue which pertains to both groups is: "to what extent
have state promotional efforts stimulated travel to the state?" Measures 3a,
3b, and 4 estimate travel to the state by Groups A and B. Measures 5a, 5b, 6,
and 7 pertain only to Group B and indicate both the number of visits and the
visitors' perceptions of the quality of state services they received. Measures
5a and 5b are similar to statistics gathered by "conversion studies" that seek
to measure the extent to which advertising coupled with information provided
by mail has stimulated travel to the state.

Data collection procedures suggested for these measures are:

(a) Estimates of the volume of tourism (Measures 3a, 3b, and 4):
These estimates would be derived from a variety of sources
described later. Several states regularly estimate the
volume of tourist travel into and within the state. These
estimates can be used as outcome measures when they reflect
the types of travel and destinations which the state seeks
to promote and, possibly, when estimates are compared to the
number of potential tourists in the market which the state
seeks to affect.

(b) Follow-up surveys of persons that received promotional
services (Measures 5a, 5b, 6, and 7): These surveys would
obtain ratings of users' perceptions of the quality of the
services, regardless of whether a trip to the state occurred,
and, possibly, estimates of the effects of the service on
their trips. A brief discussion of this survey is contained
in the third section of this chapter. An illustrative questionnaire is provided in Appendix C.

An important aspect of tourism advertising is the "image" of the state
as a tourist destination. Measures 5b and 6 provide an indication of a
state's image, but these measures consider only potential travelers who have
expressed an initial interest by responding to state advertising. The image
perceived by others is more difficult to measure. It can be done by surveying
persons in potential tourism markets or by in-depth interviews of potential
travelers, but such detailed assessments are probably most appropriate to
special studies conducted in target market areas and are not discussed further
in this report.[1]

---

1. For an example of a survey of persons in potential tourism markets,
see D'Arcy-McManus, Inc., State of Missouri Tourism Advertising Experiment,
Second Wave Analysis (St. Louis, Mo.: Missouri Tourism Commission, 1975).

Detrimental Effects of Tourism

Attention should also be given to the possible detrimental effects of tourism. Some factors of possible concern include traffic congestion, air and water pollution, loss of peace and quiet, trail erosion or loss of wildlife in natural areas, and vandalism. Instead of specific measures of the many potential detrimental effects, it is suggested that they be examined by periodic special studies of areas heavily patronized by tourists. It should be remembered, however, that the list of measures for annual monitoring shown in Exhibit 9 does not contain a measure of possible detrimental effects.

Definition of "Tourist" and "Traveler" for Analytical Purposes

Definition of the terms "tourist" and "traveler" is basic to analysis of state tourism promotion efforts. The U.S. Travel Data Center has classified the various definitions now being used into six categories:[1]

(a) Definitions based on geography: include anyone visiting the state from outside.

(b) Definitions based on purpose of trip: delineate "tourist" or "traveler" on the basis of a nonbusiness or pleasure-oriented purpose for a trip.

(c) Definitions based on miles traveled: define the trip by its length, usually more than 50 to 100 miles away from home.[2]

(d) Definitions based on time away from home: usually keyed to whether or not the visitor stayed at least overnight.

(e) Definitions based on mode of travel: separate travelers by type of vehicle used, such as private automobile or commercial common carrier.

(f) Combination definitions: include definitions which are based on more than one of the above categories.

---

1. Suzanne D. Cook, "A Survey of Definitions in U.S. Domestic Tourism Studies" (Washington, D.C.: U.S. Travel Data Center, 1975). See also Arthur D. Little, Inc., Tourism and Recreation: A State of the Art Study (Washington, D.C.: U.S. Department of Commerce, Economic Development Administration, 1967).

2. The Census Bureau's National Travel Survey uses a definition based mainly on distance from home but including other qualifying factors: ". . . all travel to a place at least 100 miles away from home . . ." excluding commuting to and from work, travel for normal daily activities, student trips to school, and trips as part of the operating crew on a train, plane, bus, or truck. U.S., Department of Commerce, Bureau of the Census, Census of Transportation, National Travel Survey, 1972 (Washington, D.C, 1973), Appendix A.

The type of definition used usually depends on which type of travel activity is being analyzed (e.g., in-state travel/travel from outside the state; camping/motel; recreation/convention) and the purpose of the analysis. These differences influence data collection procedures. For example, if an analyst were estimating spending by travelers from within and from outside the state, the receipts of a broader range of businesses would be included than if only travelers from outside the state were of interest.

The appropriate definition will also be influenced by the methodology available for gathering data. For example, some studies have based calculation of the number and origin of travelers on registration logs at roadside information centers. Such lists, however, probably include only a very limited segment of the traveling public rather than a representative group of all travelers to the state.

It is not necessary to standardize the meaning of "tourist" and "traveler" for all analytical purposes. Differences are probably unavoidable due to the different analytical problems and limitations in data collection procedures. It is important, however, that the meaning of terms be clearly stated and used consistently and that implications of different terms be explicitly considered in interpreting results.

For convenience, "traveler" and "tourist" are used interchangeably throughout this report.

Individual Outcome Measures of Tourism Promotion Activities

1. Estimated number of jobs directly related to tourism.

2. Estimated dollar amount of tourist expenditures.

Tourism-related employment (Measure 1) probably represents the more significant of these two measures in relation to state economic development. The amount of tourist expenditures (Measure 2) is included because it represents an impact which is not fully reflected by the number of tourism-related jobs. For example, businesses which provide services to travelers often operate below capacity. An increase in tourist expenditures may benefit these businesses by reducing average costs, which is worthwhile even when no increase in employment occurs.

The main use of data on employment and expenditures is to indicate tourism's effects on the state's economy. For this purpose data are presented on the state as a whole. However, for the purpose of monitoring the outcome of specific promotional services, these data should be disaggregated to:

(a) Indicate changes over time and differences among substate regions, which are related to differences in the volume of the types of tourism which the state seeks to affect. Annual data on substate regions would reflect the impact of special events, attractions, and promotional activities which may temporarily alter the distribution of tourists among areas of the state. They may also reflect the impact of state promotional efforts which emphasize particular regions for reasons related to economic development (such as a need to improve poor economic conditions in areas lacking an industrial base or a need to increase utilization of existing public facilities or businesses).

(b) Reflect the relative impacts of different target groups of tourists (conventioneers, outdoor recreation enthusiasts, interstate travelers) on the state. Since, to some extent, these groups use different facilities (particularly types of lodging) it may be possible to form categories of firms which coincide with the types of travelers served. This would allow analysis of changes in employment and expenditures related to state promotional target groups.

To meet these criteria, calculation of these measures should only include data on expenditures and employment related to the types of travel which the state program seeks to stimulate. This is likely to result in measurement data which somewhat understate the total economic impact of tourism, but it will be more capable of showing year-to-year changes in types of tourism.

Data Collection Procedures

It is quite difficult to estimate accurately the magnitude of tourism-related employment and expenditures. The tourism industry is itself difficult to delineate; it consists of businesses whose only commonality is that they serve "tourists" or "travelers" in some manner. Furthermore, the meaning of "tourist" or "traveler" (as noted above) varies according to use.

Tourism-related expenditures within states have been estimated by one or more of the following methods:[1]

(a) Use of receipts by classes of industries which serve travelers or tourists;

(b) Extrapolations from direct observations or interviews of tourists regarding their in-state expenditures;

(c) Use of the amount by which per capita sales or purchases of certain goods in the state exceeded national per capita purchases of the same goods and services; and

(d) Use of estimates of nationwide tourism-related expenditures, with the state's share of tourism estimated as a proportion of the total.

---

1. For a summary of various techniques used in tourism measurement see Arthur D. Little, Inc., _Tourism and Recreation_.

Of these methods, the first is the most widely used and seems to be the one most easily adapted for monitoring purposes. It can be used as a basis for estimating both employment (Measure 1) and expenditures (Measure 2). Since this procedure is complex and has many variations which may be appropriate for individual states, and because the literature describing this method is already extensive, only a general discussion is presented here. The method consists of two general steps:

(1) Formation of a list of tourism-related industries, and

(2) Collection of statistics on employment and expenditures in selected industries. Employment data are available by industrial class from state employment security agency records. Expenditure data can be obtained from gross tax receipts records in most states.[1]

Many states use this method to determine the total economic impact of the travel industry. Estimates are based on highly detailed lists of industries. A typical list might include such categories as:[2]

> Gasoline Service Stations
> Eating and Drinking Places
> Hotels, Rooming Houses, Camps, and Other
>   Lodging Places
> Automotive Repair Shops
> Motion Picture Theaters
> Theatrical Producers
> Bowling Alleys and Billiard and Pool
>   Establishments
> Commercial Sports
> Transportation by Air
> Hunting and Trapping and Game Propagation
> Fish Hatcheries
> Taxicabs
> Intercity and Rural Highway Passenger
>   Transportation

---

1. For a more detailed description of the method see Edward T. O'Donnell, An Essay on Methods of Measurement of Employment Directly Generated by Tourism in Massachusetts in 1958 through 1963 (Boston: State of Massachusetts, 1969); and Douglas C. Frechtling, "A Model State Continuing Travel Research Program," a paper presented to Discover America Travel Institute, Educational Seminar for State Travel Officials, 30 June 1975, at Ohio State University. Statistics on employment and expenditures are also collected by the Survey of Business conducted every five years by the Census Bureau. See U.S. Bureau of the Census Mini-Guide to the 1972 Economic Censuses (Washington, D.C, 1973).

2. This is a partial list taken from a "model" list of "primary travel-serving businesses." [U.S. Travel Data Center, Washington, D.C., n.d.]

Terminal and Service Facilities for Motor
    Vehicle Passenger Transportation
Deep Sea Foreign Transportation
Deep Sea Domestic Transportation

Because this list is designed to estimate employment and expenditures due to the travel industry in general, it may be too broad for monitoring promotional activities aimed at a specific type of traveler. For example, "Terminal and Service Facilities for Motor Vehicle Passenger Transportation" encompasses many businesses whose primary function is to help local residents travel elsewhere. The list does not exclude either business travel (business travelers may not be a target of state promotional activities) or use by local residents (e.g., of recreational facilities).

Such broad categories do not seem appropriate for monitoring purposes. Instead, states might use the following steps to form a list of industries more closely related to their promotional programs:

(a) Define the group of tourists which the state program seeks to attract. This general description would require analysis of the focus of state promotion—whether it is aimed at influencing business travelers, state residents on day trips, interstate travelers passing through the state, or some other group. This step is intended to exclude types of travelers which are not within the general scope of state promotion.

(b) Identify target groups of tourists. These are groups toward which the state directs specific promotional efforts (e.g., winter sports enthusiasts), and thus are subgroups of the general groups defined in (a).

(c) Identify types of businesses which primarily serve tourists in each of the groups defined in (a) and (b).

In defining the businesses for (c), much care should be taken to include those most closely related to the types of tourists identified in (a) and (b). Some classes of businesses related to tourism also serve local residents. However, since monitoring focuses upon annual changes and regions of the state rather than upon total state economic impact, inclusion of locally oriented businesses in the data will not be misleading unless the economic health of local businesses fluctuates substantially from one year to another due to local factors unrelated to tourism, such as population growth.[1] It is crucial to include only those businesses whose volume would fluctuate in direct response to changes in the volume of tourism. At its most extreme, this list might include only overnight facilities (motels, hotels, and camping

---

1. Where adjustments are necessary, some guidance can be gained from the procedures used in some studies to separate local from travel-related employment and expenditures. These procedures have been based on seasonal variations in expenditures, surveys of individual firms, or various "rules of thumb." See Arthur D. Little, Inc., Tourism and Recreation, pp. 17-30.

facilities). Even though lodging facilities appear to account for only 21 percent of tourist expenditures, changes in the amount of use of such facilities may reflect changes in volumes of the types of tourists related to the promotional program, depending on which groups are defined in (a) and (b) above.[1]

The method described here is similar in many respects to methods traditionally used for estimating the total impact of tourism on a state's economy. Thus, guidance can be obtained from several existing studies.[2] The modification suggested here, however, has not yet been tested.

3a. Estimated number of tourists who visited the state from target tourism markets.

3b. Estimated percent of potential tourists who visited the state from target tourism markets.

The likelihood that potential tourists will visit the state varies to some extent with their closeness to the state and their personal characteristics. Many promotional campaigns are directed at the audiences most likely to respond.

This measure is designed to indicate the success of a state's promotional program in attracting visitors from "target tourism markets"--areas which have a high potential for travel into the state.

Measure 3a estimates the number of tourists who visited the state from these target markets. Measure 3b states Measure 3a as a proportion of the potential total number of tourists. Measure 3b is the preferable form because it adjusts for the effect of changes in the population of the target market. However, Measure 3a apparently has greater feasibility because the very low percentages which are likely to occur using 3b cause difficulties in distinguishing fluctuations from year to year and because of inaccuracies which are introduced in estimating the number of potential tourists.

Although similar measures have occasionally been used in special studies, this approach has apparently not been used by any state for regular monitoring. The number of tourists is actually an intermediate outcome, since creation of employment and income is the ultimate objective of tourism promotion and employment and income effects do not vary uniformly with number of tourists.

---

1. Ibid, p. 17.

2. See O'Donnell, Methods of Measurement: Vacation Travel Business in New Hampshire (Concord: New Hampshire Department of Resources and Economic Development, 1962); and Ronald Bird and Frank Miller, Contributions of Tourist Trade to Incomes of People in Missouri Ozarks (Colombia, Mo.: University of Missouri, 1962) for examples of such studies.

A weakness in both Measures 3a and 3b is that they do not reflect the length of the visit to the state or the amount expended. Instead, they give equal weight to all visits. A special study based upon interviews of travelers (discussed below) might be used to add outcome information on this dimension.

Data on Measures 3a and 3b should also be broken down by target areas since each area presents distinct problems for state planners due to differences in accessibility and other factors. Although these measures focus on interstate travelers, they can be adapted to intrastate travelers, as discussed below.

Data Collection Procedures

The first step in obtaining data on these measures is to delineate target tourism markets. These are likely to include at least the major population centers within, say, a one-day drive from important tourist attractions in the state. More distant areas which are also potential target areas because of their climate, historical relationship, or recreational needs might also be included as part of the potential market.[1]

Measure 3a requires calculation of the number of travelers into the state from the target tourism markets (Step 1 below). Measure 3b requires the additional step of estimating the number of potential tourists (Step 2 below).

Step 1: Estimating the number of persons visiting the state from target tourism markets.

It is difficult to calculate the actual number of tourists. Less important than fine precision is comparability of annual estimates (so that significant changes can be detected) and the use of a method that focuses on the types of travelers which are the targets of state tourism promotion.

The following are four methods for estimating the number of tourists:

(a) Counts from guest registers at roadside information centers. Many states, including North Carolina and Georgia, have used registrations at roadside information centers to estimate the number and origin of travelers. The advantage of this method is that it allows identification of travelers' origins without requiring either special data collection or inconvenience to travelers. However, only a portion of travelers, and possibly only a very small portion, use these centers. Also, visitors to these centers are not likely to be representative of all travelers to the state. The accuracy of estimates based upon

---

1. North Carolina, for example, has identified parts of the northeastern seaboard region of the United States and eastern Canada as target tourism markets.

such records should be validated by a special study based on a method (such as roadside interviews) which can distinguish travelers by key characteristics (especially trip purpose) to ascertain the degree to which users of roadside centers are typical of all the types of travelers which the state seeks to attract.

(b) Survey of license plates. Several states, including North Carolina and Oklahoma, have estimated origins and other characteristics of travelers by recording the license numbers of a random sample of vehicles crossing state boundaries. For Measures 3a and 3b, recording the state of registration would be sufficient where target travel markets coincide with an entire state, and where all types of travel (including pass-through and business-related travel) are of interest. Where the target market includes an area smaller than an entire state (such as a metropolitan area), it would be necessary to obtain a more specific trip origin. In some studies this information has been obtained by checking vehicle registration records and using the owner's address as a proxy for trip origin. To determine trip purpose it would be necessary to contact a sample of drivers through roadside interviews (method c) or by mailing a questionnaire to a sample of vehicle owners to gather data on purpose and other aspects of the trip.[1]

(c) Roadside interviews. Several states have used roadside interviews to gather data on traveler characteristics, including trip origin. Florida, for example, has conducted such surveys annually.[2] This method is more costly than the methods described above because it involves stopping vehicles. Roadside interviews would probably be an unnecessarily costly method for annual monitoring of these measures alone.

(d) Counts of use of overnight facilities, such as motels, campgrounds, and hotels. These can provide data from which to estimate the volume of tourism and the origin of travel within the state. These data can be obtained by a survey of such facilities. This method has the advantage of being able to distinguish among trip types (based on type and location of facility), but it does not cover day trips.

---

1. This method was used as part of the North Carolina 1973 Travel Survey (Raleigh: Department of Natural and Economic Resources, 1974). See that study for an illustration of one method of drawing such a sample.

2. See, for example: Florida Tourist Study: 1961-1966 (Tallahassee: State of Florida, n.d.) and North Dakota, State Highway Department, Planning and Research Division, North Dakota Tourist Survey of Out-of-State Visitors: Technical Report (Bismarck, March 1972).

The methods also differ in the type of information they are capable of obtaining at one time. Methods a, c, and d can add an on-site interview or written questionnaire to obtain information on trip purpose, distination, traveler characteristics, and recreational interests. Method b can make these distinctions at the same time only by combining with method c or using a subsequent follow-up.

Because of these limitations, the method(s) selected for estimating Measure 3a should be carefully chosen in accordance with the types of tourists which the state program seeks to attract. For example, method d would be best suited to monitoring the outcome of a convention promotion program. A combination of the methods could be used for a more general promotion program, depending on the resources available for data collection and the types of information desired.

Step 2: Estimating the number of potential tourists.

A measure of potential tourists can only be an approximation; exact counting would be expensive and difficult, if possible at all. It is important, however, particularly for comparisons over time, that the method of estimating be the same each year.

The first step in estimating the number of potential tourists is delineation of "target tourism markets" as described above. Rather than considering the total population of these areas as potential tourists, a more realistic estimate might be derived by estimating only the number of people with personal characteristics which make them likely to travel to the state. Such characteristics can be identified through the special marketing studies conducted on behalf of goverment or private promotional organizations, studies of characteristics of present visitors, tourism marketing literature,[1] or by use of the travel survey conducted by the Census Bureau every five years.[2]

As noted above, Measures 3a and 3b would normally be applied to interstate, rather than intrastate, travelers. Travel from outside the state is of greater interest because it has the effect of increasing total state income. However, many states promote intrastate tourism as a method of redistributing income within the state or as a means of developing economically depressed areas. States can adapt these measures to indicate the results of intrastate promotion. Intrastate target areas (origins) and promotable attractions (destinations) must first be identified by reference to the state's goals. An estimate of the

1. See, for example, Robert W. McIntosh, Tourism Principles, Practices and Philosophies (Columbus, Ohio: Grid, Inc., 1972); Arthur D. Little, Inc., Tourism and Recreation; James M. Rovelstad, "Analytical Measures of Travel and Tourism for States and Smaller Areas: The West Virginia Model," West Virginia University Business and Economic Studies, vol. 12, no. 2 (Morgantown, W.Va.: West Virginia University, Bureau of Business Research, July 1974).

2. U.S., Department of Commerce, Bureau of the Census, National Travel Survey, 1972.

number of actual tourists could be developed using surveys at destination areas (such as convention center parking lots) or guest registers at intrastate tourist attractions. The number of potential tourists in target areas could be calculated in a manner similar to that listed in Step 2.

---

4. Number of persons who visited the state as participants in tourism-related events sponsored or substantially assisted by the state government.

A tourism promotion program may include sponsorship of, or assistance to, annual events or special attractions which either draw tourists into the state or cause them to extend their visits. These state activities may include recruitment of conventions, sponsorship of special events, and arrangement of prepackaged tours. Measure 4 would estimate the initial effect of these promotional efforts. Because of the diversity of programs which may attract visitors, it is advisable to list these data in categories (e.g., conventions, fairs, packaged tours). Data might also be disaggregated by substate region.

This measure will estimate the impact of such events more accurately if it is in the form of "number of traveler days spent in the state . . . ." However, as discussed below, this form entails additional data collection difficulties.

Data Collection Procedures

This measure requires tabulation of the number of persons attending special events and programs sponsored or assisted by the state.

It may be difficult to define a standardized threshold of effort which constitutes a "substantially assisted" role because of the variety of events and the many different sponsoring organizations which may be involved.

If Measure 4 were stated as "number of traveler days spent in the state . . . ," it would be necessary to calculate the duration of visits to the state (including time spent elsewhere than at the special event). One method would be to survey users of state-sponsored travel opportunities, asking them about the duration of their stays.

5a. Number and percent of households that requested tourism assistance from the state that later visited the state.

5b. Number and percent of households that requested tourism assistance from the state and that indicated that they visited the state at least partly as a result of the assistance which they received.

The purpose of these measures is to estimate the impact of state tourism advertising and information services on visitation to the state.[1] Data on Measure 5a have been gathered by many states by means of questionnaires sent out after receipt of tourist inquiries. These questionnaires are rarely used to estimate the impact of state assistance on tourists' travel plans, as called for in Measure 5b.

Many states evaluate the impact of tourism advertising by counting the travel inquiries received in response to advertisements. These data probably give an incomplete indication of the effectiveness of advertising because it cannot be assumed that the number of inquiries is directly proportional to the number of trips which eventually results from the advertising. Such a proportional relationship does not appear to exist for two reasons:

(a) Some persons visit the state in response to advertising without sending a request for further information;

(b) The plans of those who send inquiries are likely to be influenced to some degree by the information provided by the travel information service, in addition to the impact of the original advertisement.[2]

Measures 5a and 5b indicate the result of the advertising and travel information together, both the ability of advertising to stimulate interest and the effect of mailed information provided in response to inquiries. Advertising directed at a distant state may obtain a small response relative to nearer states, just as inappropriate, ill-timed, or unattractive travel information is likely to reduce both the number and percent of tourists who actually visit the state subsequent to an inquiry.

----

1. This measure is discussed here as it pertains to a state service which provides promotional literature by mail in response to inquiries. This measurement approach could be used to monitor several other types of assistance which are provided directly to potential tourists upon their request. For example, roadside information centers encourage longer visits and direct visitors to certain state attractions. A sample of visitors to these centers could be identified from registration logs and surveyed by the questionnaire and survey method suggested here.

2. A review of several studies by state tourism agencies of trips to the state by persons who received mailed travel information showed wide variations in the percentage of persons who later visited the state. These studies used different methodologies and were conducted in different years. One study, for example, showed that inquirers from different states varied significantly (from 44 percent to 66 percent) in proportion to those who visited the state after requesting literature. Ketchum, MacLeod, and Grove, Inc., "Survey from Among Persons Requesting Travel Information from Commonwealth of Pennsylvania" (n.p., January 1971), p. 18.

Measure 5a includes all contacts which were followed by a trip to the state. It rests on the assumption that if a trip followed receipt of information, trip planning was positively influenced to some degree by the information.

By disaggregating measurement data a state may use these measures to analyze tourism promotion efforts:

(a) By location of respondents' residences, to indicate effectiveness in attracting travel from various target markets;

(b) By type of recreational activity in which the respondent expressed an interest, to indicate effectiveness in attracting various types of recreationers;

(c) By characteristics of the respondent which relate to the likelihood of a visit to the state, to array outcome data by the estimated "difficulty" of affecting trip planning;

(d) By level of respondent's rating of the quality of tourism information, to indicate relationships between visits and perceptions of the quality of promotional services;[1] and

(e) By media through which the respondent heard about the service (e.g., magazine, newspaper), to help evaluate the results achieved by various media.

Most of these disaggregations would add to the costs of data collection because a larger number of total responses to the survey would be required to secure reliable subsample estimates.

Tourism advertising often is designed to provide a positive image for the state as a recreational destination. Questions can be included on the survey discussed below to ascertain respondent impressions of the state after viewing advertisements and mailed information. However, the survey suggested here would obtain responses only from persons exposed to state advertising. The image perceived by a broader public could be tested by market surveys, which are not discussed in this report.

Data Collection Procedures

Data for these measures would be collected by a follow-up survey of persons who received assistance from the state travel service. This survey is discussed in the next section of this chapter. Appendix C contains an illustrative questionnaire.

Collection of data for Measure 5a is relatively straightforward. What is to be determined is whether the respondent visited the state as a tourist after

---

1. Measure 7 focuses on quality of service ratings.

receiving information from the state. Question 4 in Appendix C is designed to obtain this information.[1]

Measure 5b requires respondents to assess the influence of the state's assistance on their decision to visit the state. A combination of Question 4 and Questions 6(a) through 6(c) in Appendix C can be used to gather this information.[2] Respondents may have difficulty providing accurate assessments of their reasons for visiting or not visiting the state, and this may affect the validity of the information. To our knowledge, no validation tests of such questions have been undertaken. Validation testing would likely be difficult and expensive. However, if the questionnaire and questionnaire procedures are carefully formulated and pretested, it seems likely that respondents will answer to the best of their ability.

> 6. Number and percent of households that requested tourism assistance from the state and that indicated that they have not yet visited the state for a reason which the state might have influenced.

A household's decision on whether or not to visit in the state is influenced by a wide variety of factors, many of which are personal in nature. However, considering the large number of tourists in any given year, these factors are likely to fall into fairly definite categories. Some of these include:

(a) Availability of particular recreational opportunities in the state;

(b) Overall variety of recreational opportunities in the state;

(c) Existence of unique attractions;

(d) Availability of overnight accommodations;

(e) Cost, distance, and ease of travel to desired recreational locations; and

(f) Personal resources available for leisure activities.

---

1. Examples of other surveys which used similar approaches are contained in: Arch G. Woodside, "Advertising Campaign Conversion Study, 1972" (Columbia: Department of Parks, Recreation, and Tourism, State of South Carolina, Summer 1973); City of Chicago, "Market Research Program" (Chicago: Convention and Tourism Bureau, Tourism Division, 1972).

2. Examples of other surveys which used similar approaches are contained in Massachusetts, Department of Commerce, "1962 Massachusetts Vacation Travel Study" (Boston: August 1973); Ketchum, MacLeod and Grove, Inc., "Persons Requesting Travel Information from Pennsylvania."

Some of the above can be influenced by state promotional programs; others such as personal resources cannot. Measure 6 focuses on those factors which might be influenced by the state. As with Measures 5a and 5b, methods of gathering data on this measure are based on a survey of persons making requests for state tourism information.[1]

For analytical purposes, several disaggregations of the data might be considered. These would include:

(a) Separation of data by geographical location (respondent's residence) to help determine where distance was a factor. Grouping data into about three general groups of distance would probably be sufficient for this purpose.

(b) Separation of data by type of recreational activity in which the respondent expressed an interest. This would help to interpret responses from persons stating that they were "not interested in available activities."

(c) Separation of data according to respondents' ratings of the quality of tourism information.[2] This would indicate whether a correlation exists between satisfaction with assistance provided and trips to the state.

Data Collection Procedures

Data for this measure would be collected by the same survey of a sample of persons who used state tourism information services as used for Measures 5a and 5b. Questions such as 9(a) and 9(b) in Appendix C can be used to obtain data on this measure.

The major difficulty in designing a question for this measure and in interpreting responses is that households base their decisions not merely on the attractiveness of a state but also on the state's attractiveness relative to other states. For this reason, it is probably advisable to try to determine which alternative destination was selected if the state conducting the survey was not.

This question is handicapped by validity problems similar to those involved in Measures 5a and 5b. These are primarily the difficulty (and possible unwillingness) that respondents are likely to have in stating their reasons for selecting particular travel destinations.

---

1. Other than mailed travel assistance, this measure seems more difficult to adapt to monitoring state promotional services than Measures 5a and 5b. However, Wisconsin used a follow-up survey to evaluate the services offered by a "walk-in" information center located in another state (Chicago, Illinois). This study revealed user dissatisfaction with lack of information on accommodations and on the availability of campsites where pets were allowed, and with the center's inability to make reservations.

2. Responses on quality of service are discussed in Measure 7.

> 7. Number and percent of households that requested tourism assistance
>   from the state that rated the services which they received as "fair"
>   or "poor."

This measure monitors the quality of state promotional services which
provide direct assistance to potential tourists. The significance of this
measure is that it assesses service quality from the perspective of users of
services.

An implicit assumption is that if state travel assistance conveys a
favorable impression and is properly adapted to the interests of the user,
users will decide to visit the state or extend their visits. Therefore, high
ratings by users of the quality of travel assistance is a desirable program
outcome. Even if assistance does not lead to a trip, states will not want
their assistance to leave users with a poor impression of the state and its
service.

This measure can be applied most readily to two particular services, the
mail information service and roadside information centers. It can also be
used for monitoring other promotional services which provide assistance directly
to potential tourists.

Data on this measure might be disaggregated by whether or not the inquirer
visited the state subsequent to receipt of the information requested, as determined by data on Measure 5a.

Data Collection Procedures

Assessing the mail information service. Feedback on the quality of
service provided in response to tourist inquiries by mail would be gathered
by the follow-up survey also used for Measures 5a, 5b, and 6.

Service characteristics which might be monitored include:

(a) Timeliness of the state's response to the tourist inquiry;

(b) Relevance of promotional material to tourists' interests;

(c) Attractiveness of the material;

(d) Overall helpfulness of the assistance in trip planning.

Assessing roadside information centers. The quality of roadside information centers could be rated by tourists during their visit to the centers or,
preferably, in conjunction with the follow-up survey. An alternate method for
assessing at least some characteristics is to have state personnel make ratings.
For example, Tennessee conducted a program audit of its tourism promotion in

1973.[1] During visits to roadside centers, state personnel used a five-point scale to rate such features as:

(a) Availability of tourism information (local and statewide attractions, private tourism attractions, maps, etc.);

(b) Cleanliness, state of repair, and adequacy of restrooms, telephones, water fountains, and picnic facilities;

(c) Attitude, knowledgeability, appearance, and availability of staff members; and

(d) Maintenance of structure and grounds (litter, lawn care, drainage, building repair, etc.).

Assessing other promotional services. Users of other promotional services, such as state travel agencies or assistance to persons attending conventions, might be asked to rate the assistance by means of a questionnaire administered either at the event or during a follow-up contact.

Tourism Follow-up Survey

Measures 5a, 5b, 6, and 7 rely on data collected by a tourism follow-up survey. Appendix C contains an illustrative questionnaire designed to gather data for these measures. Questions could be added to it to identify such information as types of trips made to the state, dollars spent per day, types of facilities used, size of party, and demographic characteristics of users.[2]

Ideally, this survey would be conducted at some specified time after the tourist has had an opportunity to visit the state after receiving a brochure. Several states have investigated the duration of trip planning and have found that most tourists begin planning less than six months before their trip, although the length of this period varies by season of the year. For example, a study of travel to South Dakota found that:

Approximately 50 percent of the out-of-state visitors during the non-summer months of the study indicated that they had spent less than one week in planning their trip. 40 percent stated that they had spent from one week to under six months or more. Of the out-of-state visitors during the summer months, 34 percent had spent over six months planning their visit to South Dakota. Another 37.5

---

1. Tennessee, Comptroller of the Treasury, Audit Report: State Program for Tourism Development (Nashville: 30 June 1973).

2. The questionnaire in Appendix C has not been tested, although many of the questions are based on similar surveys in South Carolina, Massachusetts, Texas, and Pennsylvania.

percent spent from one week to under six months planning their trip. Only 7.5 percent spent less than one week planning their trip.[1]

This suggests that the questionnaire should be administered approximately six months after literature is sent to prospective tourists.

The questionnaire is designed to be administered by mail, telephone, or a combination of the two. Mail surveys depend on voluntary response and therefore tend to achieve a relatively low initial rate of response. A review of approximately twenty mail tourism surveys conducted by state governments showed initial response rates ranging from 11 percent to 35 percent. Response rates were increased by a second or third request.

Telephone surveys have at least three advantages over mail surveys:

(a) They can obtain response rates which are significantly higher than by mail if initial nonrespondents are called a second or third time. Reaching respondents is not likely to be a major problem if the survey is conducted at suitable hours, such as the evening.

(b) They can be completed in a short amount of time, while mail surveys may take from four to six weeks.

(c) More detailed questions and longer questionnaires can be used.

On the other hand, telephone surveys are more costly than mail surveys.[2] Costs probably can be kept within feasible limits, however, if only a random sample of clients is sought. The advantages listed above may warrant a telephone survey in some cases.[3] An option is to use a combination with telephone contacts used to contact nonrespondents from the initial mailing to increase the overall response rate. (Though possessing many of the same advantages of telephone interviews, in-person interviews are not likely to be feasible, given the costs of travel to interview respondents scattered widely outside the state.)

---

1. Consulting Services Corporation, South Dakota Non-Resident Travel and Recreation Survey (Seattle, Wash., June 1967), p. 11

2. Based on the calculations for an in-state survey presented in Chapter 1, the average cost of fifteen-minute telephone interviews was calculated at $15 per interview if conducted by contract and $5.79 if conducted in-house. The cost of an in-house mail survey was $4.00 per questionnaire.

3. Pennsylvania used the telephone for a 1970 tourism survey. It appears that a more detailed response rate and the opportunity to probe for reasons for responses were advantages gained. Ketchum, MacLeod, and Grove, Inc., "Persons Requesting Travel Information from Pennsylvania."

The survey discussed here would be conducted on an ongoing basis, using regular department employees if possible. A routine survey procedure might involve the following steps:

(a) Interviews would be conducted each week or questionnaires would be mailed each week to households which had received tourism literature six months earlier.[1]

(b) In addition to first-time contact of users, a second attempt would be made to contact persons who had not responded to questionnaires mailed, say, three weeks before or who had been telephoned unsuccessfully during the previous week.

(c) Data from the responses would be tabulated and analyzed quarterly or semi-annually.

An ongoing procedure has two major advantages. First, interviews conducted as a routine office procedure eliminate periodic disruption of office work and the cost of hiring temporary employees to conduct interviews every six months. This, however, assumes that existing staff would be able to fit the survey tasks into their regular activities. Second, data from ongoing follow-ups are likely to have greater accuracy than if they were conducted at semi-annual intervals because all respondents are contacted at equal durations after they received state services.

If mail questionnaires are used, they can be mailed routinely on a date six months after the tourism literature was sent to the household. This procedure could be made a part of the workflow of assembling and mailing tourism literature.

Use of the telephone as the means of initial contact would probably not fit as easily into the workflow because it requires some interviewer training and verbal skills not required for assembling and mailing literature. Furthermore, it might be necessary to conduct some proportion of the telephone interviews in the evening to insure a sufficient number of responses, thereby requiring an adjustment of work schedules if regular employees are used.

A key issue, of course, is the number of questionnaires needed for annual monitoring. For random samples to estimate percentages of response to plus or minus five percentage points at an 80 percent confidence level, a minimum of

---

1. The number of interviews or questionnaires to be administered per week depends upon whether all or a random sample of users are contacted and the number of callbacks or second requests for response which are necessary. If random sampling were used, an average of 7 to 10 interviews or questionnaires per week would be necessary, assuming (a) a total desired response of 170, (b) a 50 percent initial response rate, and (c) that responses ultimately received are random. These assumptions need testing.

about 164 responses would be needed.[1] If no disaggregation of data were needed this could be the total number of positive contacts needed per year. However, it probably would be necessary to attempt interviews of more than 164 respondents for two reasons:

(a) Not all persons who receive a questionnaire will reply. If, for example, a 50 percent response rate is anticipated, at least 328 questionnaires should be sent. (This assumes that nonrespondents are typical of those who do respond. This assumption should be tested by making special efforts to contact a group of nonrespondents and comparing their responses with those from earlier respondents.)

(b) There should probably be a minimum of 100 responses sought for each of the major analysis categories. For example, if separate analyses are to be made of campers and motel/hotel users, enough questionnaires should be sent to obtain this number of responses from each of the two groups.

The selection of households to be contacted may be done through random sampling of all requests for information, unless the total number of requests is sufficiently small to allow contact with all households. Random sampling is particularly appropriate as a means of reducing the total cost of telephone interviewing.

Whether the questionnaire is administered to a random sample or to all users, the representativeness of the sample becomes questionable if the rate of nonresponse is too large (for example, over 50 percent). In such cases, additional callbacks (for telephone surveys) or requests for response or telephone contacts (for mail surveys) would be needed to reduce nonresponse rates to more acceptable limits.

---

1. Based on calculations presented in Chapter 1. Sending a questionnaire to every third person requesting travel literature is a routine procedure which might be considered.

Chapter 4

OUTCOME MEASURES FOR EMPLOYMENT AND TRAINING PROGRAMS

Employment and training programs contribute to state economic development goals by improving the skill level of the available work force and the earning capacity of individual citizens. These programs also often aim at increasing the employment of those groups within the state that have particular difficulties in achieving employment. States provide several types of employment and training programs, including remedial education, work experience (e.g., summer youth experience, adult work experience), classroom training, on-the-job training, and apprenticeship. This chapter presents some practical approaches which a state might use to monitor the outcomes of these programs.

Exhibit 10 lists the outcome measures discussed in this chapter. These measures focus on improvements in the employment status and economic well-being of individual participants as well as on participants' perceptions of the quality of program services which they received. Few states regularly gather these data at present. The measures and associated data collection procedures presented here represent a starting point, but considerable additional effort is needed to develop the procedures for regular use by state or local agencies.

These measures do not attempt to measure the noneconomic effects of employment and training programs on individuals such as on improved health.

Key Measurement Issues

Several key outcomes of employment and training programs are emphasized in this chapter.

Measures of postprogram employment and earnings status (Measures 1 to 6). States rarely determine the income or employment status of participants after they leave a program. The number of weeks of employment and the earnings levels (including public assistance) achieved by former participants are key postprogram data now lacking. The "quality" of postprogram employment, such as participants' job satisfaction, should also be assessed.

In addition to ascertaining the postprogram status of former participants, it is desirable to identify the degree of improvement in earnings and employment resulting from the program. Measures 1b, 4b, and 5b are included as estimates of change in participants' earnings and employment. Much of this change,

EXHIBIT 10

SUGGESTED OUTCOME MEASURES FOR EMPLOYMENT AND TRAINING PROGRAMS

Objective	Suggested Measure	Data Collection or Estimation Procedures
Improve employment status of participants	1a. Number and percent of former participants who were employed at least "x" weeks in the six months (or one year) since termination[a]	Follow-up survey of former participants
	1b. Percent change in the average number of weeks of employment in the six months (or one year) before participation versus the six months (or one year) after termination for former participants as a group[b,c]	Follow-up survey of former participants
	2. Number and percent of former participants employed in a job related to the training provided by the program at six months (or one year) after termination	Follow-up survey of former participants
	3. Number and percent of former participants who rate their employment status at six months (or one year) after termination as "excellent" or "good"	Follow-up survey of former participants
Improve earnings of participants	4a. Number and percent of former participants who received at least "x" dollars in earnings in the six months (or one year) since termination[d]	Follow-up survey of former participants or government tax or other records of earnings
	4b. Percent change in the average earnings in the six months (or one year) before participation versus the six months (or one year) after termination for former participants as a group[b,c]	Follow-up survey of former participants or government tax or other records of earnings
	5a. Number and percent of former participants who are "self-supporting" (not receiving government subsidy) at six months (or one year) after termination	Follow-up survey of former participants

EXHIBIT 10 (CONT'D)

Objective	Suggested Measure	Data Collection or Estimation Procedures
Improve earnings of participants (cont'd)	5b. Percent change in the number of former participants who are "self-supporting" at six months (or one year) after termination versus six months (or one year) before participation[b]	Follow-up survey of former participants
Improve the skill level and/or work-related attitudes of participants	6. Number and percent of former participants who demonstrate at least a minimum skill or attitudinal improvement at program exit as compared with program entry	Standardized testing at the beginning and end of program
Minimize low quality service	7. Number and percent of former participants who rate key aspects of services as "fair" or "poor"	Survey of participants and dropouts (at termination or in a follow-up survey)
Provide services of sufficient magnitude, type, and accessibility to meet the needs of the adult population	8. Number and percent of total adult population who are in need of program services but are not being provided with services (by type of program)	Socio-economic population data; data on population being served; statewide survey of households
	9. Number and percent of adults who are in need but who have not applied for program services due to reasons which the state can influence	State-sponsored survey of households
	10. Number of applicants eligible for program services but not enrolled within "x" weeks[e]	Program records

[a]"x" represents a preselected number of weeks, such as twenty.

[b]Ideally, data on this measure would be stated relative to similar data on a comparison group.

[c]For these measures, average employment and earnings before and after the program (stated in absolute rather than percentage terms) are also of interest and should be stated along with data for the measure listed.

[d]"x" represents a preselected amount, such as the total amount someone would earn if paid at the federal (or state) minimum wage rate full-time for six months (or one year). For year-to-year comparisons, adjustments should be made in "x" to reflect cost of living changes.

[e]"x" represents a preselected number of weeks defined by the government, such as four. Different numbers of weeks may be appropriate for different types of programs.

however, may be caused by factors other than the program, such as general economic conditions, age, and family responsibilities of participants.

These measures do not attempt to specify the degree of change attributable to the program. In some instances, program effects can be partially isolated by comparing the degree of change (Measures 1b, 4b, and 5b) for participants with the degree of change experienced by similar "comparison" groups of non-participants.[1]

Comparison groups could be formed by drawing a systematic sample from the general population of program applicants who are eligible but who ultimately do not participate in the program or from a list of enrollees who drop out of the program at an early stage. However, the utility of such comparison groups in regular program monitoring is impeded by several factors, the most important of which are the difficulty of identifying a truly "comparable" group of nonpartici-pants and the problems of obtaining data regularly on members of the comparison group.[2] The Social Security Administration Continuous Work History Sample, or the earnings file of the state unemployment insurance agency, offer some possible sources of comparison groups and data on them, but they provide data on earnings only. Other types of data (e.g., employment status and other aspects of work history) would probably be obtainable only by special contact with nonparticipants. The difficulty of locating and interviewing nonparticipants is likely to make this very costly.

Another method of determining the impact of certain factors unrelated to the program is by comparison of measurement data for different groups of par-ticipants. For instance, the influence of age on program results might be partially indicated by grouping measurement data according to participants' ages. Methods of grouping outcome data for analytical purposes are presented in the third section of this chapter.

Ideally more preferable is the procedure of randomly assigning some persons to the program (the "experimental" group) and others to a "control" group that are given no services (or a different kind of service). However, this procedure in general requires considerably more effort and may not always be feasible. Nevertheless, we do recommend that such "controlled experiments" be considered, especially to evaluate potentially very expensive programs. The measurement procedures discussed in the report should also be useful in such experiments.

---

1. "Comparison" group is suggested rather than "control" group because the latter implies random selection of participants, normally not feasible in public programs.

2. A comparison group consists of persons with characteristics similar to those of program participants who did not participate in the program. Key characteristics would be those which correlate to a significant degree with potential success in the labor market, such as age, wage level, race, and preprogram duration of unemployment. See John H. Goldstein, "The Effectiveness of Manpower Training Programs: A Review of Research on the Impact on the Poor," in Benefit Cost and Policy Analysis (Chicago: Aldine Publishing, 1972), pp. 348ff.

For an excellent discussion of sources for and relative advantages and weaknesses of comparison groups, see Enar Hardin, "On the Choice of Control Groups," in Michael E. Borus, ed., Evaluating the Impact of Manpower Programs (Lexington, Mass.: Lexington Books, 1972), pp. 41-68.

We recommend that data for the measures proposed here be obtained by a follow-up interview of former participants (including dropouts) at specific times, such as six or twelve months after program exit. A long enough period is needed to reflect longer-term effects and not merely, for example, the participant's employment status at the time of exit from the program. Conversely, a period longer than one year lessens the timeliness of outcome data to officials for annual budgeting and planning purposes and also makes it more likely that factors other than the employment or training program will occur and significantly affect the former participant's employment situation. Even one year, however, is not long enough to show the full long-term impact of a program. Occasional in-depth studies can be used to assess longer-term impacts.

The recommended follow-up survey can be conducted by mail, telephone, in-person, or a combination of methods. To reduce costs, a random sample rather than all former participants might be included in the survey. During this project an illustrative set of questions for this survey was developed with the assistance of the states of North Carolina and Wisconsin. This set is presented in Appendix D. It has not been fully tested, although limited testing of some questions was undertaken in North Carolina during the summer of 1976.

Two other methods are available if resources for interviewing a large number of former participants cannot be obtained:

(a) Contact with employers. In this method initial contact is made with the participant's first postprogram employer, also at some period such as six or twelve months after the participant's exit from the program.

(b) Use of data from government records. This method utilizes unemployment compensation or social security records of former participants to gather both preprogram and postprogram earnings data.

Procedural issues associated with each of these three methods are discussed in the last section.

Measure 6, change in participants' skill and employment attitude level, should be considered more of an "intermediate outcome" rather than a measure of "final" outcome. Changes in skill levels (or attitudes) do not in themselves guarantee that employment will be found by participants or that job satisfaction will follow. The measure is included here because of the considerable interest in it often expressed by program officials.

Measures of participant perceptions of the quality of program services (Measure 7). Few states gather data on participants' perceptions of the quality of program services. Measure 7 relies on participant ratings of such factors as the extent to which the program helped the participant to find or keep a job, the accessibility and convenience of services, the clarity of instruction, the courtesy and empathy of program personnel, and overall satisfaction with the program. These ratings can indicate reasons for lack of success, problems which affect specific groups of participants, and other operational problems which might warrant more detailed investigation.

Participant ratings of the helpfulness of programs in finding and keeping a job would need to be obtained in a follow-up interview. Data on other aspects of the quality of service could be added to either a termination or follow-up interview. Perception data should also be obtained from program dropouts, since dissatisfaction may explain their failure to complete the program.

Measures of unmet need (Measures 8, 9, and 10). The extent to which program services are reaching those in need appears to be an aspect of employment and training programs which is often neglected.[1] Obtaining estimates of the total number of persons in need of services can be a very difficult task. Unemployment, income, and other data on substate regions discussed in Chapter 1 can provide a starting point for estimating unmet need, but much developmental work remains to be done in this area.

Establishment of client difficulty and other external influence categories. Two important types of factors which affect program results should be considered in analyzing and interpreting outcome data, especially data on employment and earnings status. These are case difficulty and other external influences.

There can be very substantial differences in the ease with which participants achieve successful outcomes. Therefore, in order to make fair assessments and to provide meaningful information to policy makers, it appears advisable to classify participants in categories of case difficulty. Research on which characteristics denote potential participant difficulty is far from complete, but such characteristics as education, race, age, and previous job experience probably affect the likelihood of a participant's postprogram success. Because of the difficulty of identifying and quantifying factors which contribute to case difficulty, the selection of elements forming the basis for categorization would initially have to be based on judgments by state program staff, perhaps with the advice of outside experts. Classification procedures could be based on information obtained at intake.

Such categorization would also permit analysts to (a) establish separate targets for groups with different degrees of difficulty, (b) provide guidance for the allocation of resources among these groups, and (c) permit state officials to distinguish changes in success rates due to changes in the mix of participants or due to different mixes of participants in different programs.

Other external factors, such as local unemployment rates or the rate of growth of employment, also affect the ability of former participants to obtain or to hold employment. In a regular monitoring system it is not possible to control for all, or even many, external factors, but provision can be made for considering a few potentially important factors, at least partially.

---

1. The CETA local planning process recognizes the importance of this aspect and requires an attempt by state and local governments to identify groups with special service needs. Few jurisdictions, however, have been able to quantify, and on a regular basis monitor, the magnitude of need for particular program services, due to a lack of suitable data.

Specific procedures for dealing with case difficulty and other external factors were neither identified nor given initial testing in this project. Future research to provide guidance to states on factors which might better delineate difficulty classes and other external factors is highly desirable. These issues, however, seem sufficiently important to warrant implementation of even rudimentary procedures.

Classification for case difficulty and other external factors is discussed more fully later in this chapter.

Individual Outcome Measures for Employment and Training Programs

1a. Number and percent of former participants who were employed at least "x" weeks in the six months (or one year) since termination.[1]

1b. Percent change in the average number of weeks of employment in the six months (or one year) before participation versus the six months (or one year) after termination for former participants as a group.[2]

2. Number and percent of former participants employed in a job related to the training provided by the program at six months (or one year) after termination.

3. Number and percent of former participants who rate their employment status at six months (or one year) after termination as "excellent" or "good."

4a. Number and percent of former participants who received at least "x" dollars in earnings in the six months (or one year) since termination.[3]

4b. Percent change in the average earnings in the six months (or one year) before participation versus the six months (or one year) after termination for former participants as a group.[4]

---

1. "x" represents a preselected number of weeks such as twenty. Data gathered for this measure could also be tabulated in other ranges, such as no weeks, less than 4 weeks, 4 to 13 weeks, and 14 to 26 weeks of employment.

2. Ideally, data on this measure would be stated relative to similar data on a comparison group. For this measure, average employment before and after the program (stated in absolute, rather than percentage, terms) is also of interest and should be stated along with data for the measure listed.

3. "x" represents a preselected amount, such as the total amount someone would earn if paid at the federal (or state) minimum wage rate full-time for six months (or one year). For year-to-year comparisons, adjustments should be made in "x" to reflect cost of living changes.

4. Ideally, data on this measure would be stated relative to similar data on a comparison group. For this measure, average earnings before and after the program (stated in absolute, rather than percentage, terms) are also of interest and should be stated along with data for the measure listed.

5a. Number and percent of former participants who are "self-supporting" (not receiving government subsidy) at six months (or one year) after termination.

5b. Percent change in the number of former participants who are "self-supporting" at six months (or one year) after termination versus six months (or one year) before participation.[1]

Measures 1a, 4a, and 5a consider only participants' employment and earnings status since leaving the employment or training program. Measures 1b, 4b, and 5b, on the other hand, are comparative; they attempt to estimate the degree of change in duration of employment and amount earned before versus after participating in the program.

Single time-period measures (Measures 1a, 4a, and 5a) can be used, but by themselves they do not indicate the degree to which participants' postprogram status differs from their preprogram status. They merely show whether a desired postprogram status (such as employment, earnings level, self-sufficiency) has been achieved. It would appear that the comparative measures are preferable to the single time-period measures because the former indicate improvement over preprogram status. However, the comparative measures have important limitations and can be misleading. Some of their problems are as follows:

(a) Preprogram data may be difficult to obtain. Revised intake forms and procedures are likely to be needed if the preprogram information is to be obtained from the participant at intake (when the information will be freshest in the participant's mind). If obtained from the participant at the follow-up period (as provided for in the follow-up questions illustrated in Appendix D), the former participants may not be able to recall their work history accurately. Other data collection approaches (such as that which gathers some data from employers) do not provide preprogram data.

(b) New members of the labor force lack a preprogram work history on which to base preprogram versus postprogram comparisons.

(c) The possibility of misinterpreting preprogram versus postprogram earnings data can occur if participants may have had a high level of employment and earnings before a national or local recession. Postprogram employment, even if not at the same earnings level, could represent a significant success for the program even though postprogram earnings were actually lower.

(d) In any event, changes from preprogram to postprogram work history are influenced by many factors apart from the program. Differences in labor demand before and after the program and changes in participant characteristics during participation (e.g., increased age or family responsibilities) can affect the likelihood that there will be changes in postprogram employment status.

1. Ideally, data on this measure would be stated relative to similar data on a comparison group.

Our suggestion is, if resources permit, that states obtain both preprogram and postemployment data and prepare a "change score" as called for in Measures 1b, 4b, and 5b. Measures 1a, 4a, and 5a should be estimated, with or without Measures 1b, 4b, and 5b.

Systematic comparison of the employment and earnings records of participants with a similar group of nonparticipants (comparison group) can also be undertaken to estimate the degree of change attributable to program participation. As discussed earlier, however, the development of comparison groups raises complex analytical issues which are probably beyond the scope of regular monitoring. The next section suggests that internal comparison groups (similar groups of participants) may serve as a partial alternative.

Measure 2 indicates the degree to which the benefits of training are being utilized at six or twelve months after termination. It applies only to programs which contain a training component. This measure assumes that employment related to the training provided by the program represents a benefit derived from participation. The measure suggested here assesses only the job held by the participant at the time of postprogram contact, rather than each job since program exit. The measure could be expanded to include the entire postprogram period by stating it as "number of weeks of employment in training-related jobs in the six months (or one year) since termination."

Measure 3 consists of former participants' ratings of their satisfaction with their job status at six months or one year after termination. Some officials may not consider client job satisfaction as a legitimate outcome of employment and training programs, or as only a very secondary outcome.[1] However, we suggest that some officials will consider it an important outcome. Also, it is correlated with employment stability and so the information on satisfaction might be a useful proxy for stability. In addition to asking former program participants for ratings of overall job satisfaction, they might also be asked to rate more specific aspects of their current employment, such as their perceptions of advancement opportunities and utilization of their skills.

Data Collection Procedures

Collection of Data on Preprogram and Postprogram Employment and Earnings (Measures 1a, 1b, 4a, 4b, 5a, and 5b)

These measures require data on former participants' work history and earnings for a specified time period since their termination from the program. "Termination" as used here includes both exit upon completion (graduation) and exit prior to completion. Persons who drop out voluntarily or who do not complete the program for some other reason should be included for a complete assessment of what happened to program entrants.

The simple method of considering dropouts is to include them in the base when calculating percentages for outcome measures but to exclude them in the

---

1. A concise discussion of the role of participant attitudes in evaluation of employment and training programs is contained in Harold L. Sheppard, "The Value of Attitude and Opinion Measures in Manpower Evaluation Research," in Borus, ed., Evaluating Manpower Programs, pp. 83ff.

follow-up survey of former participants, thereby considering them "nonsuccesses." However, this method may be unfair to the program because many noncompletions are for reasons which do not necessarily reflect negatively on the program, such as ill health, military service, or taking a job. An alternative is to include in the base of percentages only noncompletions which are recorded as "nonpositive." It is highly preferable, however, to collect actual data from dropouts as well as graduates, even though it is probably more difficult to locate and interview dropouts.

A general description of procedures for gathering preprogram and postprogram data is presented here. A more detailed discussion is contained in the final section of this chapter.

The length of the postprogram period for these measures should be at least six months after termination to reflect impact but probably no greater than one year after termination so that data can be available for annual budgeting and planning purposes. The preprogram period used in Measures 1b, 4b, and 5b should be at least six months and preferably as long as one year. (12-month periods for both pre and post data have the advantage of avoiding seasonal employment effects, but begin to strain respondents' recall abilities and for postprogram information will make it more difficult to locate the former participants.)

Three sources might be used for gathering data on postprogram employment and earnings of former participants:

(a) The participant,

(b) The initial postprogram employer,

(c) Government records.

We recommend method (a). To gather data from participants, a questionnaire could be administered by mail, telephone, or personal interview. Unless a mail survey is used, only a representative sample of former participants is likely to be feasible. Participant interviews can provide data on all employment, earnings, and perception measures (1 through 5 and 7). If preprogram data are not available from another source (such as from intake interviews), such data can be gathered along with postprogram data in the follow-up interview. For programs shorter than three months, use of a follow-up contact six months after program exit would require the respondent to recall work history and earnings for slightly more than one year (six months after exit, six months before entry, plus the program period). This seems feasible in view of the recent experience of the Census Bureau in conducting the Continuous Longitudinal Manpower Survey (CLMS). For longer programs, however, the recall period may become so long as to jeopardize the accuracy of preprogram data. It is advisable that questionnaires which requirelong recall periods be carefully pretested and validated. Follow-up interviews of participants have the additional advantage of being able to provide data on perceptions, such as those called for by Measures 3 and 7.

Method (b), obtaining data from the initial employer, provides data only on postprogram work history and earnings (Measures 1a and 4a). Furthermore, it is likely to miss employment history for any individual that had employment with firms other than the one which employed the individual at the time of initial postprogram employment and which is recorded in the participants' records. Arrangements would have to be made with the government agency controlling the records to obtain data without violating privacy regulations. This method may not be feasible for monitoring programs where large numbers of former participants tend to enter types of employment excluded from reporting requirements. For example, earnings from most public employment are not reported to social security files. In addition, such records may not present the data in the most desirable way. For example, earnings data in unemployment compensation records may be presented only as quarterly totals. Preprogram, program, and postprogram periods may not coincide with such quarters but may overlap them.

In addition to using the follow-up survey to gather preprogram data, such data might be gathered at or soon after intake by state personnel. This method would shorten the length and reduce the complexity of follow-up interviews. However, at least two problems must be overcome before this method can be used for regular monitoring:

(a) Preprogram data needed for outcome measurement are not now generally gathered at intake. For example, data gathered on persons enrolled under the federal Comprehensive Employment and Training Act (CETA) at intake include labor force status, number of weeks unemployed, and estimated annual family income immediately prior to entry. These data do not match the needs prescribed by measures recommended in the report. For example, labor force status at entry would probably overstate unemployment for the preprogam period because unemployment of participants tends to be highest immediately prior to entry.[1] Some of the measures recommended here are also related to individual earnings rather than annual family income.

(b) Data gathered at intake may contain a reporting bias due to the tendency of applicants to overstate recent unemployment and understate income in order to meet eligibility requirements. This reporting bias has not been fully verified, but could be investigated locally by comparing data reported in the past with wage data contained in state unemployment compensation or income tax records.

Collection of Data on Degree of Postprogram Employment Use of Training (Measure 2)

The purpose of a "use of-training" measure is to determine the extent to which skills gained through a program are being utilized in postprogram jobs. Since this may be difficult to determine without detailed analysis of job activities, ratings should be made in categories such as "probably used training," "possibly used training," "probably didn't use training" and "unable to determine."

---

1. Westat, Inc., Characteristics of CETA Participants, p. 1-11.

Two methods can be used for making this assessment:

(a) Categorization based on job descriptions. Ratings would be based either on verbal or written descriptions of major job duties, job title, or class of occupation as designated by the dictionary of occupational titles. Such basic information might be gathered from former participants during interviews using a question such as Question 5 in Appendix D, or from the employer.

(b) Perceptions of former participants. The perceptions of former participants regarding the degree to which their job utilizes program-related skills has been used by many surveys as a means of evaluating use of training. A question such as Question 6 in Appendix D might be used for this purpose.

Collection of Data on Former Participants' Satisfaction with Postprogram Employment (Measure 3)

Questions to gather data for Measure 3 would be included in the six-month (or one year) participant follow-up survey. Employee satisfaction with various aspects of employment could be rated, including utilization of skills, prospects for advancement, wage level, and overall satisfaction. A much wider variety of characteristics has been included in special studies,[1] but, only two or three probably need to be included for purposes of regular monitoring. Questions 6 (on utilization of skills), 7 (on overall job satisfaction), and 8 (on opportunities for advancement) in Appendix D can be used to obtain these data.

---

6. Number and percent of former participants who demonstrate at least a minimum skill or attitudinal improvement at program exit as compared with program entry.

This measure quantifies the degree of change related to programs which seek to improve skill or educational levels and programs which seek to improve participants' work habits or adaptation to work environments. Skill and attitude changes are "intermediate" outcomes because they do not necessarily lead to improved employment or income. The assumption, however, is that improvements in skill and attitude are closely related to potential employment success.

Measure 6 determines the number of graduates who demonstrate a minimum degree of improvement, as shown by their scores on standardized tests administered at entry and at termination. This number would be stated as a percent of the total number of entrants.

---

1. David J. Weiss et al., "Manual for the Minnesota Satisfaction Questionnaire," Minnesota Studies in Vocational Rehabilitation: XX (Minneapolis: University of Minnesota, Industrial Relations Center, 1967).

Data Collection Procedures

Two problems warrant special mention:

(a) Availability of tests. A 1973 survey shows that more than 140 different tests are available for assessing employment-related skills and attitudes; this survey could be used by states before they select tests for monitoring their own programs.[1] Tests used should be consistent with the skills or attitudes which the program seeks to improve.

(b) Possible bias of tests. Many of the available instruments are traditional written tests which may distort the scores of certain population groups or persons who do not read well. Efforts have been made to develop tests which are more appropriate for such groups, but validation of these newer tests is incomplete.[2]

Because different tests are likely to be used in assessing different types of programs, opportunities for comparing different programs by this measure will be limited. Whenever possible, however, the same standardized test should be used for similar programs.

The participants who do not attain a minimum skill or attitudinal improvement include dropouts who may have participated only briefly in the program,[3] and graduates who, though fulfilling all requirements, failed to show minimal improvement. Because this latter group reflects directly upon the substance of the program, the percent of graduates who fail to show minimal improvement should probably be stated separately.

---

7. Number and percent of former participants who rate key aspects of services as "fair" or "poor".

This measure consists of participants' ratings of various aspects of program services. Although participant perceptions do not directly indicate improved income and employment status, low levels of satisfaction may reduce the ultimate success of the program and may even adversely affect the attitudes of participants. In addition, these data provide a means of identifying program problems. For example, although a program may be achieving improved employment and earnings status, its operation may be demeaning, highly inconvenient, or otherwise detrimental to participants.

---

1. U.S., Department of Labor, Manpower Administration, Methods of Assessing the Disadvantaged in Manpower Programs: A Review and Analysis (Washington, D.C., 1973), pp. 143-45.

2. Ibid., pp. 132-35.

2. Those who did not complete the program for reasons which do not reflect adversely on the program might be excluded from this group. Such reasons might include ill health.

Multi-level ratings are recommended for this measure, such as "excellent, good, fair, or poor" or "very satisfied, somewhat satisfied, somewhat dissatisfied, or very dissatisfied."

Aspects of the program which are rated may vary somewhat, according to the type of program and the population served. General characteristics which might be rated are:

(a) Extent to which the program helped the participant to find and keep a job;

(b) Clarity of training materials;

(c) Clarity of project instructions;

(d) Accessibility of project services;

(e) Convenience of project services (e.g., hours of operation);

(f) Courtesy of project personnel;

(g) Interest and empathy shown by project personnel;

(h) Availability of transportation and other auxiliary services (child care, etc.);

(i) Overall attitude of project personnel; and

(j) Overall quality of project services and training offered.

Each of these characteristics can be considered as a separate performance measure.

Data Collection Procedures

Data on the program's helpfulness in getting and keeping a job would have to be obtained in the follow-up interview. Other perception data might be gathered at the time of program completion or as part of the follow-up interview six to twelve months after termination.

Obtaining perception data at or near the time of termination eliminates the need to locate and interview former participants and avoids memory problems. In general, the data should not be gathered by program personnel, who, in effect, are being assessed, to avoid biasing the participants' responses. Confidentiality of responses is necessary here (as with all the responses given in the follow-up survey) to protect the respondents.

Perception questions in the postprogram follow-up survey allow former participants to provide a longer term reflection on the helpfulness of the program, particularly in relation to their present employment status. However, perceptions of the program will probably be influenced somewhat by participants' experiences in the job market since leaving the program. It is suggested that perception data gathered at the follow-up interview be disaggregated according to current employment status.

Another difficulty is that at six to twelve months after termination the participant will be less able to provide detailed responses. This time lag may also make this feedback less useful in program planning.

An illustrative set of questions for obtaining data on aspects of service quality other than helpfulness in getting and keeping a job is presented in Exhibit 11. If these data are gathered by a follow-up contact, questions from Exhibit 11 could be adapted and included in the follow-up questionnaire in Appendix D. Appendix D includes two questions for obtaining data on helpfulness in getting (Question 17) and keeping (Question 18) a job.

---

8. Number and percent of total adult population who are in need of program services but are not being provided with services (by type of program).

The preceding measures all address the outcomes regarding persons that have entered employment or training programs. This measure attempts to estimate systematically the proportion of the total state population or particular client groups (such as residents of various substate regions or in various disadvantaged groups) who are in need of service and are not being served.

Data Collection Procedures

The "population in need," defined by such general characteristics as income level and employment status, can be estimated by a statewide survey such as that described in Chapter 1. Specifically, the percentage of respondents who are unemployed, or working part-time while desiring full-time work, or whose earnings are below specified levels can be estimated by the responses to Questions 4 through 15 of Appendix A.

This unmet need could be estimated for (a) one point in time, particularly the time of the interviews; (b) the full preceding 12-month period; or (c) both. This information could be obtained for only the respondents or for all adults in the households surveyed. At a minimum, we suggest that information be obtained on (a), the status at time of the interviews, and preferably for all adults in the households surveyed. Questions 7 through 14 can be used to identify those currently in need. Questions 4 through 6, 16, 18, and 20 can provide unemployment and earnings information for the previous year (there is no information on part-time employment for the previous year).

These questions provide a count of the percent of adults in surveyed households who were unemployed, employed fewer hours per week than they would prefer, or employed at low earnings levels. The percent could be applied to the total

EXHIBIT 11

ILLUSTRATIVE QUESTIONS FOR GATHERING PARTICIPANT
PERCEPTIONS OF TRAINING PROGRAMS[a]

1. I am going to list several types of manpower staff with whom you had contact. Could you tell me **generally** how satisfied you were with the help they provided. Please tell me whether you were very satisfied, somewhat satisfied, somewhat dissatisfied, or very dissatisfied. [Note: Titles are for illustration only. Titles actually used should be typical of personnel in local programs.]

	Very Satisfied	Somewhat Satisfied	Somewhat Dissatisfied	Very Dissatisfied
Intake Personnel/Receptionist	____	____	____	____
Instructors	____	____	____	____
Counsellor/Placement Personnel	____	____	____	____

2. I will list for you some possibly negative characteristics of (name of program). Please tell me how often you **actually** encountered these characteristics by saying often, sometimes, or never.

	Often	Sometimes	Never
Training materials difficult to understand	____	____	____
Program instructions difficult to understand	____	____	____
Difficulty getting to the program (transportation)	____	____	____
Program personnel not courteous	____	____	____
Hours of operation of the program inconvenient	____	____	____

3. (For pretest only) Are there any other problems you encountered that I have not mentioned?
_____

_____

4. Generally how satisfied were you with the attitude of the staff of the project?

Very satisfied ____
Somewhat satisfied ____
Somewhat dissatisfied ____
Very dissatisfied ____

5. How would you rate the overall quality of training materials?

Excellent ____
Good ____
Fair ____
Poor ____

6. Hou would you rate the overall quality of the program services which you received?

Excellent ____
Good ____
Fair ____
Poor ____

[a]Many of these questions are adapted from the Continuous Longitudinal Manpower Survey (CLMS) of the Census Bureau. They are designed to gather information for Measure 7 in Exhibit 10.

adult population in the state to estimate the total number of adults in need in the state. For Measure 8, however, additional information is needed to distinguish those who are in need but who are receiving services from those who are not receiving services. Measure 8 focuses on the latter group.

Data on the number of adults currently being served by employment and training programs might be obtained through agency records and could then be subtracted from the estimated total number of adults in need in the state as derived from questions in the survey. Probably a better option is to obtain the estimate of those not being served from the survey. Respondents would be asked whether they were currently in an employment and training program. Exhibit 12 illustrates questions to obtain such information.

Ideally, this population in need would be further classified by various characteristics believed to affect employment or earnings status, such as skill level, extent of education, past work experience, extent and severity of physical problems, and access to child care. Question 3 in Exhibit 12 would provide data for such a classification. Three questions in Appendix A would also provide information for classifying reasons for unemployment or part-time employment: Question 6 for persons unemployed during the previous year; Question 11 for persons employed part-time during the previous week; and Question 14 for persons unemployed during the previous week.

> 9. Number and percent of adults who are in need but who have not applied for program services due to reasons which the state can influence.

This measure attempts to estimate the incidence of nonapplication for program services by eligible persons for reasons which the state can potentially influence, such as:

(a) Inaccessibility of program services ("too far away," "too hard and expensive to get there" or "transportation not available");

(b) Eligible person unaware of available services or eligibility for them;

(c) Waiting list too long;

(d) Lack of child care services; and

(e) Eligible person doesn't want "public" help.

Data Collection Procedures

These data would be collected by means of the statewide survey using questions such as 3a and 3c in Exhibit 12.

One special problem with Measure 9 is that the sample for the statewide survey is drawn from all households in the state, meaning that a sufficient number of responses might not be obtained from persons potentially eligible

EXHIBIT 12

ILLUSTRATIVE QUESTIONS FOR GATHERING OUTCOME DATA
ON UNMET NEED FOR EMPLOYMENT AND TRAINING SERVICES[a]

1. During the past twelve months, have you or any adult member of this household had a problem finding a new job?

    ____Yes   SKIP TO Q3
    ____No   GO TO Q2

2. During the past twelve months, have you or any adult member of this household been refused a job because you did not have the skill, training, or schooling required for the job?

    ____Yes   GO TO Q3
    ____No   SKIP TO NEXT PART OF SURVEY

3. [ASK FOR EACH ADULT HOUSEHOLD MEMBER FOR WHICH APPLICABLE]

   (a) Did (name of household member) try to get help for this problem?

    ____Yes   GO TO (b)
    ____No   ASK: Why? [DO NOT READ RESPONSES]
           ____Applied but not eligible
           ____Unaware of how or where to obtain help
           ____No transportation
           ____Too far away
           ____Child care
           ____Ill health; disability
           ____Waiting list too long
           ____Don't want "public" help

   (b) Where did (name of household member) try to get help?

    ____State agency [SPECIFY]:_____
    ____Other

   (c) Did (name of household member) get help there?

    ____Yes   GO TO (d)
    ____No   ASK: Why? [DO NOT READ RESPONSES]
           ____Applied but not eligible
           ____Not interested
           ____Unaware of how to obtain help
           ____No transportation
           ____Child care
           ____Ill health; disability

   (d) Is this still a problem for (name of household member)?

    ____Yes
    ____No   GO TO NEXT PART OF SURVEY

[a]Developed from questions in New Hampshire, Department of Health and Welfare, "Social Service Needs Survey," (1975). Similar questions have also been included on other state surveys. For example, see Florida, Department of Health and Rehabilitative Service, "Assessment of Needs of Low Income Urban Elderly Persons" (May 1973).

for services to provide meaningful information as to reasons for nonuse of agency programs. If it is assumed, for example, that 20 percent of the households in a state have a member who is eligible for program services, a survey of 1,500 to 2,000 households would contain approximately 300 to 400 needy households (100 for each of, say, four primary geographic areas). Some of the needy households will already have utilized state employment and training programs. The result will be data from a smaller sample, increasing the likelihood of inaccuracies due to sampling.

The number of responses can be increased if increased numbers of respondents for the survey are drawn from population groups or areas likely to contain a larger proportion of eligible persons. Another alternative is to include questions for this measure on special surveys of unemployment, welfare, or social service clients.

---

10. Number of applicants eligible for program services but not enrolled within "x" weeks.

The reduction of delays in providing help to those needing and wanting help is important to the potential participant and is an appropriate government goal. Measure 10 attempts to measure progress toward this goal. The measure provides information on the backlog of applicants waiting to enter programs already filled to capacity. For the most part, this goal can be attacked by the state government which has the ability to expand capability and to regulate entries. However, external factors, such as unemployment rates, can affect the results by increasing the number of applicants.

This measure would be particularly useful if data were separated by categories of program. For example, major categories might include skill training, orientation and motivation, remedial education, public service employment, and rehabilitation.

Data Collection Procedures

Data for this measure are gathered by most programs and program referral agencies. One method of tabulating data would be to use the number of eligible persons awaiting enrollment at a specific time, such as the end of the year. More representative data would be obtained by averaging the number of persons awaiting enrollment at the end of the month, but this would require additional data collection and calculations.

Two issues are likely to affect the validity of the measurement data:

(a) The extent to which individual programs encourage, or discourage, persons from putting their names on waiting lists will likely differ among programs. In addition the currency of such lists may be in question. In addition, potential participants may be discouraged by long waiting periods. This may cause the measure to underestimate the number of persons who are eligible and who desire program services but who are not enrolled.

(b) Eligible persons may submit applications to more than one employment and training program. This may inflate the values in the measure if a method is not found to correct for such duplication.

Methods of Analyzing Data

This section discusses the need for considering variations in outcome data due to participant mix--both case difficulty and other external factors--and on differences by client group, region, program type, and program operator. Each of these is discussed below.

Case Difficulty

There can be substantial differences among participants in the ease with which they achieve positive results. These are referred to as differences in "case difficulty." If a project has enrolled a high proportion of the most difficult cases, its success rate should be expected, other things being equal, to be lower than that for similar projects with lower proportions of difficult cases.[1] Therefore, outcome data on participants should be separated by case difficulty to the extent possible.

Outcome data separated by case difficulty can provide a basis for (1) comparing outcome data from different programs, or changes in participant mix from one period in time to another, (2) establishing outcome targets for groups of differing difficulty, and (3) allocating resources for service to groups with differing difficulty.

Performance data should be classified into perhaps three to four general levels of difficulty. It would be expected that degree of program success would vary among these groups, assuming that each group received identical services. Exhibit 13 illustrates a display of measurement data by case difficulty.

A systematic procedure needs to be developed for classifying participants at intake by case difficulty. Three types of procedures might be used:

(a) Assignment could be done by grouping participants by personal characteristics which seem to correlate with likelihood of post-program success. This could be based solely on participant records (primarily intake records) or, as discussed in (c), it could also be based on interviewer assessment at intake.

---

1. The problem of "creaming" (selecting for training only those most employable) has been widely discussed. For example see John W. Scanlon et al., An Evaluation System to Support Planning, Allocation, and Control in a Decentralized, Comprehensive Manpower Program (Washington, D.C.: The Urban Institute, 1971). Sewell also notes that some job training programs, such as Manpower Development and Training Act (MDTA) and On-the-Job Training (OJT), had eligibility requirements that led to applicant rejection rates as high as 65 percent. See David O. Sewell, "Critiques of Cost-Benefit Analyses of Training," Monthly Labor Review (September 1967), p. 45.

EXHIBIT 13

ILLUSTRATIVE DISPLAY OF OUTCOME DATA BY LEVELS
OF CASE DIFFICULTY[a]

Level of Case Difficulty	Number of Cases	Percent of Former Participants Employed at Six Months After Termination in a Job Related to Training, by Region of the State:			
		Coast	Mountain	Central	Total
Difficulty I	(596)	78	65	70	71
Difficulty II	(610)	52	41	61	51
Difficulty III	(602)	36	33	38	35
Difficulty IV	(580)	15	21	13	16
Total	(2,388)	42	38	47	44

[a]The numbers shown in this table are hypothetical.

Unfortunately, there appears to be little convincing evidence as to how much specific participant characteristics affect likelihood of postprogram success. The RAND Corporation developed a system of difficulty classification to provide the basis for a proposed incentive program for California state job placement agents. In this program agents were to be paid bonuses based on their success in increasing annual earnings of clients above what earnings would have been without state placement assistance. Using regressions, RAND developed a means of predicting potential success based on race, health, work experience, geographical location, and other client characteristics.[1] This method is not presently in use.

Another recent study of factors affecting the performance of the Employment Service in New Jersey found that age of clients was particularly significant. The study found higher placement rates for local offices with higher proportions of youthful clients.[2]

1. F. W. Blackwell et al., "Performance Rewards for Services to the Employable Poor: A Proposed Incentive Pay System for California Job Agents," R-1028-HRD (Santa Monica, Calif.: RAND Corporation, June 1972).

2. Fred Englander, "Factors Affecting the Performance of the Employment Service in New Jersey" (Trenton: New Jersey Department of Labor and Industry, Division of Planning and Research, 1975).

Also a 1975 study tested the feasibility of the use of biographical information across ethnic groups to predict three-month employment tenure among disadvantaged Employment Service applicants who had received no previous manpower training or counseling services and were placed by state agencies into a varying range of manufacturing and service occupations and the prediction of the completion of Job Entry among WIN program enrollees. It found age, race, and sex to have significant effects on tenure.[1]

Several social service agencies (particularly vocational rehabilitation programs) have attempted to develop procedures for assessing employability of clients at intake. Such procedures have involved the use of inventories of client characteristics, such as physical condition, mental condition, emotional functioning, social adjustment, marital adjustment, and stability of residence. The validity of these inventories as predictors of future employability has not yet been established.[2]

Based on those studies, participant characteristics which a state probably should consider include age, race, sex, educational level, criminal records, physical handicaps. preprogram earnings and work history, and standardized test scores. Participant characteristics are likely to vary in significance among programs and projects. If computer and analytical capacity is available, statistical techniques such as regression analysis of characteristics of participants' postprogram earnings can be undertaken using data on preprogram and postprogram earnings such as from the Social Security Administration wage files.[3]

---

1. Richardson, Bellows, Henry & Company, Inc., "A Report on Predicting Job Tenure Among ES Applicants and Completion of Job Entry Among WIN Enrollees Through the Use of Biographical Information," prepared for the U.S. Department of Labor, Manpower Administration (Washington, D.C., January 1975).

2. For a review of research in the area of vocational rehabilitation, including some validity testing, see William J. Westerheide and Lowell Lenhart, Case Difficulty and Client Change, Monograph 1 (Oklahoma City: Oklahoma Department of Institutions, Social and Rehabilitative Services). For the results of a test in Denver which indicated that scores on the Denver Department of Welfare's inventory of economic independence did correlate with rates of closure for AFDC cases, see Harold A. Morse, "Measuring the Potential of AFDC Families for Economic Independence," Welfare in Review (November-December 1968), pp. 13-20. An inventory similar to the one used in Denver has been used since 1972 by the Welfare Division of the Department of Human Resources of the State of Nevada. A somewhat revised version of the Denver and Nevada inventories is also currently being used by the Michigan Department of Social Services, Division of Social Services Evaluation and Analysis, in a four-state, HEW-supported, evaluation of social services funded under Title XX of the Social Security Act.

3. Such an approach was used in Edward C. Prescott and Thomas F. Colley, "Evaluating the Impact of MDTA Programs on Earnings under Varying Market Conditions," Report no. MEL-73-08 (Philadelphia: University of Pennsylvania, October 1972).

(b) A "panel of experts" drawn from inside and outside government could be asked to identify key characteristics and their weights, based on their judgments for the simple classifications suggested here.

(c) A third option is to rely on staff members to make judgments at intake about the applicant's prospects for successful training. The interviewer would integrate personal characteristics with observable factors, such as "interviewability" and potential work habits. This approach has the major long-run drawback that the classifications would not be standardized and the reliability of the assignments to classifications would be under severe question. However, in the initial year of outcome measurement, this might be the feasible approach.

Once any of these rating systems is established, its use should be periodically monitored to insure that it is applied as objectively as possible. Furthermore, application of the rating system should be monitored to insure that difficulty ratings are not influencing the selection of participants for programs, unless, of course, this is the explicit policy of the program.

Other External Factors

Inevitably, other external factors can affect program results. Among the most important are economic and social conditions, such as the extent of unemployment and numbers and types of jobs available. It is not likely to be feasible for an ongoing monitoring system to consider regularly a large number of external factors, but it is likely to be able to consider perhaps two or three.

A recent study of the performance of local employment service offices in New Jersey found these external factors significant in affecting local office placement rates: percent of employment in manufacturing, rate of growth of employment, and per capita income.[1]

There is also research on factors affecting the performance of state employment services which states may wish to consider in selecting variables for grouping substate data. The Resource Allocation Formula (RAF) which the U.S. Department of Labor uses to distribute federal funds to state employment services includes adjustments based on this research. External factors being used to allocate Fiscal 1978 funds include: size of the civilian labor force, percentage change in nonagricultural employment, average weekly earnings in UI-covered employment, state unemployment as a percent of national unemployment, population density, average size of employing establishments, and proportion of workers in major occupational groups.[2]

---

1. Englander, "Employment Service in New Jersey."

2. For more information on the Resource Allocation Formula (RAF) and the research on which it is based, see U.S., Department of Labor, Employment and Training Administration, "Guide for Application of Resource Allocation Formula (RAF) for Fiscal Year 1978," Employment and Training Handbook No. 340 (Washington, D.C., June 18, 1977).

A straightforward method of considering the impact of external influences is by disaggregating outcome data. For example, regions of the state might be classified into three to five groups, based on such statistics as unemployment rates and rate of growth of employment. Ideally, the particular statistics chosen for grouping regions of the state would be based on previous evidence that these characteristics of the local economy were likely to affect post-program employment status. However, as noted above, such information is very limited. Outcome data on local employment or training programs would then be grouped by location into these classes. Exhibit 14 illustrates a simplified form of presenting data in this way using only one statistic, the unemployment rate.

Labor market area data from the employment security agency would probably be a suitable basis for these classifications. Such substate regions would likely consist of two or more counties since most labor markets encompass an area larger than a single county.

EXHIBIT 14

ILLUSTRATIVE DISPLAY OF OUTCOME
DATA BY LOCAL EMPLOYMENT CONDITIONS[a]

Regional Unemployment Level (Annual Average for 1976)[b]	Number of Clients	Percent of clients served by programs in these regions that were employed six months after termination in a job (related to training) for former participants in:		
		Classroom Training	On-the Job Training	Both Groups
Less than 4.0 percent (Regions 2 and 6)	(310)	68	80	76
4.0 to 6.5 percent (Regions 3, 4, 5, and 12)	(716)	54	63	59
6.6 to 8.0 percent (Regions 1, 7, 8 and 11)	(924)	45	44	45
More than 8.0 percent (Regions 9 and 10)	(438)	32	35	33
Total	(2,388)	49	54	51

[a]The numbers shown in this table are hypothetical.

[b]As noted in the text, the choice of the characteristics for grouping substate regions should be based on evidence of probable effects on post-program employment status if possible. The unemployment rate is used here only to illustrate a simplified format for displaying data. There is not currently sufficient evidence to indicate whether or not this is a variable which should be used to classify substate regions.

Groupings of Outcome Data by Client Group, Program Type and Program Operator[1]

Client Group (Target Groups)

Various titles of the Comprehensive Employment and Training Act identify particular population subgroups as warranting special consideration.[2] Other target groups are likely to be identified by the particular region of the state where their program is located--perhaps those geographical regions served by particular planning councils. Disaggregation of outcome data by target group can help determine how well the programs are serving such groups.[3]

Several characteristics are currently gathered at intake, at least for CETA programs. These include age, sex, ethnic group, command of English, criminal record, physical handicaps, veteran status, number of school years completed, family income, and labor force status immediately before entry.[4]

Data can also be disaggregated by substate region. This might be useful as a means of assisting regional planning boards. Substate disaggregations may also be useful for coordinating employment and training programs with other economic development programs planned on a regional basis.

Program Type

It may be useful to compare the outcomes of different types of programs. For example, the CLMS categorizes CETA programs as public service employment,

1. Much of the following discussion on "client group," "region," "type of program," and "program operator" is based upon: Olympus Research Corporation, "Survey and Analysis of Current and Local Self Evaluation Efforts," Draft Final Report (n.p., 1975), pp. 99ff.

2. Comprehensive Employment and Training Act of 1975 (CETA) identifies the following subgroups (paraphrasing the legislation):

Title I: Disadvantaged persons, unemployed persons, and underemployed persons.

Title II: Persons who are in need of certain skills and experience in order to fill certain public sector jobs (must also be unemployed or underemployed).

Title III: Certain ethnic groups, certain age groups, and other special groups (criminal offenders, seasonal or migrant farm workers.

3. Where these measures are used for monitoring CETA Balance of State or individual prime sponsor programs, the "significant segments" identified in the program's annual plan could consider target groups.

4. Several problems may arise with regard to these data. In some programs, certain characteristics are not gathered consistently due to failure of intake interviewers to complete forms. Some items, such as family income, are not validated and may contain inaccuracies. Finally, there is evidence to show that labor force status immediately prior to entry is not representative of longer term employment history. In view of these problems, the main utility of intake forms may be in gathering data on such demographic characteristics as age, sex, and race.

employability development, direct placement, or youth work experience. Other and more narrow categories can be defined for comparing the results of similar but distinct programs, such as on-the-job training and classroom training.

Types of programs are sometimes viewed as alternate strategies toward achieving improved participant employment or income. The major purpose of comparison of outcome data by type of program is to determine the relative outcomes of various strategies.

Program Operator

Since CETA gives state and local planning bodies the option of selecting program operators, state or local officials may wish to disaggretate certain outcome data according to operators.

Two caveats should be heeded if this is done. First, there may be a very large number of program operators, thereby requiring a very large sample if comparisons among all operators are desired. A more feasible option would be to make comparisons only among the largest programs, those for which large enough samples of their participants are available to permit fair comparisons.

Second, program operators may serve groups of participants who differ greatly in difficulty and are subjected to different external influences, making it especially important that outcome data be grouped by case difficulty and, where the operators are in different localities, by magnitude of external influences.

Procedural Issues Related to Gathering Data

Measures 1 through 5 rely on data pertaining to the employment and income status of former program participants. This section discusses some additional major procedural issues in collecting these data, either by means of (a) a follow-up survey of former participants; (b) postprogram employer contacts; or (c) the use of government records, such as unemployment compensation files, state or federal income tax records, or social security records.

Follow-up Survey of Former Participants

Thus far, few states have undertaken systematic follow-up surveys of their participants, either for monitoring or for special studies. Coverage of the "balance-of-state" area in particular pose many data collection problems unanswered by previous studies, since it is largely rural, involves a variety of programs, and includes a very large geographical area. The Continuous Longitudinal Manpower Survey (CLMS) now being conducted by the U.S. Department of Labor is helpful in some respects, but its interviewing methods are far more sophisticated and costly than those likely to be appropriate for regular use by state governments and, in any case, it is in its early stages as of this writing.[1] Several agencies, such as the North Carolina Manpower Development Corporation and the Department of Labor, are developing practical guides for local follow-up surveys, but these are still largely untested.[2] Testing in this study was limited to a few questions used in North Carolina that were similar to those contained in Appendix D.

Appendix D contains an illustrative set of questions which might be used as a follow-up interview to gather preprogram and postprogram work history and earnings data. These questions gather data on:

(a) Postprogram earnings and employment status (Measures 1a, 2, 4a, and 5a),

(b) Perceptions of postprogram employment (Measure 3),

(c) Perceptions of program services (Measure 7), in which case questions such as those shown in Exhibit 11 should also be added,[3] and

(d) Data on preprogram work history and earnings (Measures 1b, 3b, and 5b).[4]

Exhibit 15 lists the questions in Appendix D which could be used to gather data for each of these measures.

Appendix D contains questions to obtain both preprogram and postprogram data in the same postprogram interview, but it can be revised to include only postprogram data. To gather these data, the questionnaire uses the approach of the CLMS, which traces work history backwards from the time of the survey. Where the program is of long duration, such as a year, the length of the recall period may be sufficiently large as to reduce the effectiveness of this method. Data gathered in a pretest of this questionnaire might be compared with government records, such as the respondent's unemployment compensation records, to ascertain whether earnings data and, by inference, employment history as

---

1. The CLMS is a survey of up to 52,000 present and past participants in CETA programs. All members of the sample are contacted twice, shortly after registration and six months later. Two-thirds of the sample are also contacted eighteen months after first receiving CETA services and one-fourth are again interviewed thirty-six months after initially receiving CETA services. CLMS does not appear suited to state or local monitoring oe valuation because the sample is not drawn to provide representative information on state or local jurisdictions.

2. "An Approach to Evaluation for Planners and Evaluators" (Chapel Hill, N.C.: North Carolina Manpower Development Corporation, May 1975); and "Employment and Prime Sponsors" (Washington, D.C.: U.S. Department of Labor, 1976).

3. As discussed under Measure 7, data on perceptions of program services could also be gathered when the participant terminates the program. If so, data on helpfulness in keeping a job would not be available and data on helpfulness in getting a job might be more limited.

4. As discussed under Measures 1 to 5, preprogram data might be gathered at or soon after intake if biases in such data can be overcome.

EXHIBIT 15

QUESTIONS IN CLIENT FOLLOW-UP SURVEY (APPENDIX D)
FOR USE IN GATHERING OUTCOME DATA

Measure		Questions
Employment	1a	2, 11, 12
Status	1b	2, 11, 12
	2	5, 6
	3	6, 7, 8
Improved	4a	14
Earnings	4b	14, 16
	5a	13
	5b	13, 15
Service	7	17, 18
Helpfulness		

reported by respondents, are reasonably accurate. If not, the questionnaire
and interviewing methods would have to be improved before the procedures are
used officially. If poor recall or other factors impair the availability
or accuracy of preprogram data, monitoring might be undertaken solely on the
basis of postprogram data as discussed earlier.

Timing of The Follow-up

A basic issue pertaining to postprogram data is selection of the point
in time after termination at which to gather data. Research in the field
does not suggest any particular time as most appropriate. Instead, selection
of a time requires the balancing of several factors.

The time should be long enough after termination to allow employment
status and earnings to reflect the longer term impact of the program. A
period as short as one or a very few months would indicate only very short-
term effects of the services and might not indicate such effects as those
of seasonal fluctuation and the ability of graduates to hold employment.

On the other hand, the time period should be soon enough after termination to allow outcome data to be available for upcoming budget and planning
cycles and to minimize the difficulties of locating former participants for
interviews.

An appropriate time for a follow-up seems to be six to twelve months
after termination. While data on this period will not show very long-term
results, they will prevent exaggerated estimates of success based on status
at, or soon after, termination. All former participants should be interviewed
at approximately the same time after termination in order to obtain comparable
results.

A difficult problem, encountered in both North Carolina and Wisconsin, is that in some cases the date of termination is difficult to determine from program records. Several program operators apparently delayed recording a participant as terminated at the end of the program until it was determined whether the participant would be placed in employment or would obtain subsequent program services. The termination date which appeared in the records, therefore, was not necessarily the date on which the participant completed the program and was available for employment. To some extent this problem can be corrected by improved reporting procedures.

Another option is to undertake the follow-up of participants at some fixed period, such as six, nine, or twelve months after intake. This would avoid the problems caused by unclear termination dates. And it would avoid the confounding effect of the length of program on results--with all participants being followed-up at the same time after entry regardless of length of training program.[1]

Data on the preprogram period should not consist solely of status at entry, but should cover a period of at least several months prior to entry. Results of the CLMS indicate that the percentage of program participants who were unemployed had gradually increased as the time prior to program entry decreased. Approximately 20 percent of the participants were unemployed at twelve months before entry, 30 percent were unemployed at three months prior to entry, and 50 percent were unemployed immediately before entry. This indicates that status at entry may not be representative of unemployment during the six or twelve-month period prior to entry. A period of at least six months, and preferably twelve months, prior to entry would give a more accurate representation of pre-program earnings and employment status.[2]

Method of Interview

Three methods of interview can be considered: mail, telephone, and in-person. A combination of the three methods may be the most appropriate approach. Assuming proper training of interviewers, a combination of any or all three methods does not seem to bias response data significantly for most types of questions.[3]

Mail questionnaires have been used in several employment and training surveys. Although mail surveys are characterized by low cost relative to other methods, this cost may be increased by the need to use telephone or personal

---

1. We have suggested this procedure for follow-up of former clients of social and mental health services. Annie Millar, Harry Hatry, and Margo Koss, Monitoring the Outcomes of Social Services, Volume 1: Preliminary Suggestions (Washington, D.C.: The Urban Institute, May 1977); and Alfred H. Schainblatt, Monitoring the Outcomes of State Mental Health Treatment Programs: Some Initial Suggestions (Washington, D.C.: The Urban Institute, May 1977).

2. Westat, Inc., Characteristics of CETA Participants, pp. I-7 and I-12.

3. Joseph R. Hochstin, "A Critical Comparison of Three Strategies of Collecting Data from Households," Journal of American Statistical Association 62, no. 315 (19 September 1967):982-83.

interviews of nonrespondents to compensate for a low initial response. A review of several surveys which used slightly different procedures (including monetary incentives) and involved different types of programs and population groups showed that variations in the response rates to mail questionnaires ranged from less than 1 percent to over 50 percent.[1] A survey of former rural job corps participants (possibly a particularly motivated group) obtained a fairly high response rate; 40 percent responded to an initial mailing and 54 percent of the initial nonrespondents replied to a second request, resulting in an overall response rate of 72 percent.[2] Another study using mailings to a disadvantaged population resulted in a 44 percent response rate, 32 percent from the first mailing and 12 percent from the second.[3] Both these studies used monetary incentives of a few dollars (five or less) per contact; the extent to which they induced responses is not clear. It appears that the population group being surveyed and the length and complexity of the questionnaire may have had a greater influence on the rate of response. Therefore, careful pretesting on a similar group is advisable before mail is selected as an initial method.

If mail is chosen, a questionnaire such as the one in Appendix D probably should not be used, since its length and complexity would discourage responses. A mail questionnaire should be limited to gathering a very few types of data for a particular date (e.g., specific week of the year), such as:

(a) Whether the respondent was employed;

(b) If employed, wage rate and number of hours in the work week;

(c) An estimate of the use of program skills in that employment (see Question 5 in Appendix D);

(d) An estimate of the number of weeks unemployed during a defined period since leaving the program; and

(e) Ratings of the helpfulness and quality of the program.

Where an insufficient number of responses is obtained in a mail survey, telephone or personal interviews of nonrespondents can be used to obtain a greater number of responses.

It is probably preferable that the entire survey be conducted by either telephone or in-person interview. Mail questionnaires are less likely to obtain needed information on work history for the postprogram period, income data, and information on the respondent's receipt of public assistance. This is due to the limited complexity of questions which can be used on a mail

1. Morgan V. Lewis, "Finding the Hard-to-Locate: A Review of Best Practices," in Borus, ed., Evaluating Manpower Programs, p. 165.

2. G. H. Miles et al., "Optimizing the Benefits of Neighborhood Youth Corps Projects for Rural Youth" (n.p.: North Star Research and Development Institute, 1969).

3. R. G. Walther, "Methodological Considerations in Evaluative Research Involving Disadvantaged Populations" (Washington, D.C.: Social Research Group, George Washington University, 1969).

questionnaire. Furthermore, the personal contact between interviewer and respondent in a personal interview can help to overcome the sensitive nature of some types of questions, particularly those on income.

Personal interviews have been used by the Census Bureau and in many special studies to collect work history and income data.[1] Many of the questions in Appendix D are adapted from Census Bureau surveys, particularly the CLMS. The Census Bureau does not use the telephone as the initial means of contact, contrary to what we suggest here. A telephone survey questionnaire similar in general respects to Appendix D was tested on twenty-nine former training program participants in North Carolina in 1976. In this test, respondents contacted by telephone responded willingly to questions about earnings and employment history, even though many respondents' last contact with the state program had been as much as two years prior to the interview.

An Alternate Approach: Contact With Employers[2]

A method being used by the Office of Manpower Resources in Baltimore obtains postprogram earnings and employment data by contact with former participants' employers at a lower cost than by contact directly with participants. If the former participant is still employed by this employer, data on the present hourly wage of the participant is obtained from that employer and an assessment is made of whether the present job is related to training, based on information from the employer. If the former participant is no longer employed by the initial employer, the former participant is then contacted directly to obtain information on hourly wages and relationship of work to training for present and all other jobs since program termination. All the Baltimore interviews have been conducted by telephone, apart from some large employers who have been contacted by mail either as a convenience or because they refused to provide information by telephone. Baltimore contacts about 200 to 300 former trainees per month. This requires the equivalent of approximately one staff month of effort each month.

Use of Government Records as a Source of Data

Records of the Social Security Administration, the state unemployment compensation agency, and the state income tax agency offer an alternate source of data for measures of employment and earnings.[3]

The federal Privacy Act forbids the disclosure of data on individuals by the Social Security Administration for these purposes. However, these federal limitations apparently do not pertain to unemployment compensation data, although state law or policy may impose similar constraints. Where individual disclosure is prescribed, data could probably be obtained on participants grouped for

1. As for example, the National Longitudinal Study, Continuous Longitudinal Manpower Study, and Current Population Survey.

2. Information on this method was provided in 1976 by the Office of Research and Evaluation of the Mayor's Office of Manpower Resources (Baltimore).

3. Final Report of the Panel on Manpower Training Evaluation: The Use of Social Security Earnings Data for Assessing the Impact of Manpower Training Programs (Washington, D.C.: National Academy of Sciences, January 1974).

purposes of analysis without violating individual privacy. The advantages and disadvantages of federal and state records as sources of data are listed in Exhibit 16.

A major difference between social security and state unemployment compensation records is the time it takes to obtain data. It is estimated that earnings data could be obtained from social security files nine to twelve months after the end of the quarter in which they were earned. The time needed to obtain data from state unemployment compensation files can range from eight to ten weeks (based on recent experience in Virginia)[1] to the three to four months needed in field tests in North Carolina.

There are also differences in the type of workers included in the files, due to differences in social security and unemployment compensation insurance coverage. With changes in coverage beginning in 1978, unemployment records will be more comprehensive as they will cover about 97 percent of the labor force.

The potential usefulness of state unemployment compensation records for the following two purposes was examined in a limited test by North Carolina:[2]

(a) As a source of follow-up information for monitoring and evaluating state employment and training programs, and

(b) As a means of validating data gathered by other means, such as data recorded by intake personnel or as reported by respondents in follow-up interviews.

For the first purpose, two issues were considered:

(a) Whether outcome measures could be formulated based on data in employee and employer records maintained by the state unemployment compensation system, and

(b) Whether these records could be adapted for the purpose of calculating such measures.

It was found that data of possible relevance to monitoring or evaluation included the following data from the employee file:

(a) Employee earnings for the five most recent quarters, listed by employer for each quarter. Earnings are posted eight to twelve weeks after the end of each quarter. Earnings for the sixth most recent and earlier quarters were not retained but could be preserved by the state employment security agency by special arrangements. Such an arrangement would require transfer of

1. Joint Legislative Audit and Review Commission, Virginia General Assembly, "Program Evaluation: Virginia Drug Abuse Control Programs" (14 October 1975).

2. This test was designed and conducted by personnel in the North Carolina Department of Administration during 1976. They received excellent cooperation from the state Employment Security Commission and the state Office of Employment and Training.

EXHIBIT 16

ANALYSIS OF GOVERNMENT RECORDS AS SOURCES
OF EARNINGS AND EMPLOYMENT DATA

Advantages

● Cost is estimated to be small compared to field surveys.[a]

● Data included are accurate. They contain neither interviewer bias nor interviewer error. While there may be some degree of reporting error due to mistakes in the reports of employers, this is not viewed as significant, especially in its effect on manpower evaluations.

● Earnings from several time periods are available. Thus, problems with inaccurate recall of past earnings are absent.

● Data could also be obtained on persons not in employment and training programs, by providing the social security numbers of nonparticipants. Thus, participants could be compared with nonparticipants or with the one percent sample of the master file (Continuous Work History Sample) based on the demographic characteristics contained in the file (race, sex, age, and income).

● Social Security Administration records contain data on earnings, regardless of the state in which they were earned. (A state using its own unemployment compensation records will have no record of out-of-state earnings.)

Disadvantages

● Earnings are reported without any record of changes in hours of work or wage rates. Earnings are reported only quarterly, so if for example a person entered a program in the middle of a quarter, earnings for that quarter could not be disaggregated into preprogram and postprogram earnings.

● The records provide no explanation of the reason for zero earnings, which may be due to any one of the following causes: the worker was not in the labor force; the worker was in the labor force but unemployed; the worker failed to earn a minimum amount (for SSA data, $50) from any single employer per quarter; the worker was employed in a noncovered occupation.

● The records do not cover all occupations. About 10 percent of all workers nationwide are in noncovered occupations, including farm work, most federal, and some state and local jobs. An evaluation of Manpower Development and Training Act (MDTA) programs found that relatively few trainees were employed in these occupations and the proportion of uncovered participants was less than 10 percent.[b] However, with increased coverage of unemployment compensation, employment not covered in these records will decrease to about 3 1/2 percent of the labor force on January 1, 1978.

● Earnings above the current maximum of $15,300 per year are not reported for social security purposes. For purposes of unemployment compensation, earnings of less than $100 per quarter are not reported.

● No information is provided on the former participants' ratings of program helpfulness or quality. Information to use to determine whether the job is related to training is also very limited.

[a]A 1974 study reported that a computerized process for securing earnings data from social security files would cost less than ten cents per observation (Use of Social Security Earnings Data, p. 10). A limited test of a manual data collection process using enemployment compensation records was conducted in North Carolina in 1976; during this test it took an average of eight minutes of staff time to obtain earnings data on one former training program participant. (This test is discussed further in the text.)

[b]Prescott and Colley, "Evaluating Impact Under Varying Conditions."

data on selected participants from the general wage file to
another computer tape prior to routine erasure of records on
the sixth most recent quarter.

(b)   A code representing the identity of each employer, by quarter
      of employment.

(c)   The employee social security number.

Data available from the employer file included:

(a)   The employer's unemployment insurance rate (based largely upon
      the amount of unemployment experienced by the firm's past
      employees and the firm's number of years in the state).

(b)   The total payroll of the firm.

A number of variations of the measures were formulated, generally parallel
to most of the measures in the postprogram status category listed earlier
in this chapter (Measures 1 to 5). Measures which seemed most directly usable
for regular monitoring were: (a) the number of quarters in which participants
had covered earnings since the quarter in which program termination occurred;
(b) total covered earnings in the quarters subsequent to the quarter in which
termination occurred; and (c) number of quarters of employment with earnings
from jobs related to training (as estimated by the nature of the employer).

The feasibility of collecting data on these three measures from the
unemployment compensation records was tested by the North Carolina Department
of Administration. For purposes of the test, the files of sixty former participants in one classroom training program and one on-the-job training program
were used. Precautions were taken to maintain the confidentiality of these
records during the test. It was found that about one staff day was needed to
obtain data on the above measures from the files on the sixty former participants.

This test was not primarily designed to determine the validity of the measurement data gathered. However, an attempt was made to validate the data through
personal interviews of twenty-nine former participants. These interviews showed
that nearly all respondents had at least a small amount of noncovered income.
This indicates that noncovered employment may cause major discrepancies between
unemployment compensation data and actual earnings. More systematic tests
are needed before dismissing government records as a source of monitoring data,
especially in light of expanding coverage of unemployment compensation. P.L.
94-566, which will become effective on January 1, 1978, will expand unemployment
compensation coverage to employees of firms above a certain size, state and local
governments, nonprofit institutions, and several others. This will result in
unemployment insurance coverage of 97 percent of the workforce.

Sampling Procedures

Major state employment and training programs enroll large numbers of participants. Therefore, monitoring should probably be based on data collection for

a randomly selected sample, rather than all former participants. Sample size will be a less critical issue if a method which has a relatively low cost per contact (such as a mail survey or a search of government records) is used. A state may still, however, find it preferable to collect outcome data on only a portion of former participants.

The sample might be drawn at intake or early in the program. Such early sampling has two advantages. First, additional demographic data (e.g., classifying cases as to "difficulty") and additional preprogram data (work history or earnings) would only have to be gathered on those participants sampled rather than all applicants. Second, participants who do not complete the program would be included in outcome measurement. Samples drawn after termination tend to include only graduates. (It seems appropriate to include drop-outs in the follow-ups to provide more comprehensive information for assessing the program's effects.)

If the sample is drawn early in the program, precautions should be taken to avoid special treatment of the participants selected. Thus, when eligibility or referral decisions are being made, those making such decisions should not know that certain applicants are being observed for evaluative purposes. One procedure that might be used for gathering this additional data on the sample at intake is to provide those participants with postage-paid mail questionnaire addressed to the Department of Administration or some other neutral party rather than the offices of the employment and training staff.

Determination of the size of the sample needed involves questions of: (a) cost (the larger the sample, the more expensive), (b) the precision desired when comparing groups of participants (whether comparisons are made of outcomes from one year to another, or among different groups during one year), and (c) the number of groups for which comparisons are desired (each such group requires a large enough sample to provide the desired precision).

Determination of the number of groups for which comparisons are desired is an important early stage in sample size selection. Groupings might include:

(a) The four categories used by CLMS for program types: public service employment, employability development, youth work experience, and direct placement.

(b) For each program type, perhaps three to five ranges of case difficulty (for a total of 12 to 20 groups).

(c) The various planning districts in the state (for North Carolina this would be 17 and for Wisconsin 10, if both the balance of state and local prime sponsor areas were included).

(d) Groups of counties classified into three to five categories based on other external factors (such as unemployment rates and growth of employment).

In Chapter 1, a sample size of about 160 was estimated as being needed for estimating percentages within plus or minus 5 percentage points at an 80 percent confidence level. We suspect that if the sample is properly representative, even a sample of 100 is likely to give government agencies adequate precision for most uses. Thus, if five case-difficulty groups for each of four types of programs were desired, a minimum sample size of 2,000 to 3,200 would be needed. Or if comparisons among 15 planning districts were desired, a sample size of 1,500 to 2,400 would be needed.

The average cost figures listed in Exhibits 3 and 4 can be used to make rough estimates of the cost of conducting surveys of this size using alternative combinations of mail, telephone, and in-person interviews. Because the population groups involved here are generally more difficult to locate, these cost estimates may be somewhat low. As noted in Exhibit 16, search of government records is estimated to cost considerably less.

APPENDICES

Appendix A
ILLUSTRATIVE QUESTIONNAIRE FOR A STATEWIDE HOUSEHOLD SURVEY[1]

    1. OBTAIN THE NAMES OF MEMBERS OF THE HOUSEHOLD OVER 16 YEARS OLD.

M-3   2. Were there any periods of time during the past twelve months when no member of your household was employed, but at least one member was seeking work or wanted work but felt it was useless to look for work?

        _____Yes   GO TO Q3

        _____No   SKIP TO Q4

M-3   3. About how many weeks during the past twelve months did your household have no employed members, but one member was either actively seeking work or wanted work but felt it was useless to look for work?

        _____weeks   (PERMIT AN ANSWER OF "LESS THAN ONE WEEK")

    REGARDING EACH MEMBER OF THE HOUSEHOLD OVER 16 YEARS OLD, ASK THE RESPONDENT:

M-2   4. During the past twelve months, has (name of household member) at some time wished to work but not been working?

        _____Yes   GO TO Q5

        _____No   SKIP TO Q7

---

    1. These questions are illustrative only. They are based in part on the Census Bureau's Current Population Survey (CPS) and experiences of 1976 test surveys sponsored by the state governments of North Carolina and Wisconsin, undertaken as part of this project. However, the particular wording and sequence of these questions have not been adequately tested. A state wishing to use this material should test it thoroughly before determining the final form of its questionnaire.

    The number to the left of each question indicates the specific measure(s) in Exhibit 1 for which the question is to obtain data.

    This list is not in final questionnaire form. In particular, a questionnaire would need to provide space for recording (and subsequently counting) separate responses to some questions for several persons over 16 years old in the household. This would include Questions 4 through 14. Other additions would also need to be made--for example, to provide for recording "don't know" responses.

IF YES, ASK:

M-2

5. During how many weeks during the past twelve months was (name of household member) not working?[1]

    _____number of weeks

M-2

6. For what major reason was (he) (she) not working?[2]

    (WRITE APPROPRIATE NUMBER OF WEEKS NOT WORKING TO THE RIGHT OF THE REASON FOR NOT WORKING--THERE MAY BE DIFFERENT MAJOR REASONS FOR DIFFERENT PERIODS OF NOT WORKING.)[1]

    (a) Not working but seeking work[3]   _____weeks

    (b) Unable to work: illness, disability   _____weeks

    (c) Temporarily working but not seeking   _____weeks
        work; slack work; layoff; labor
        dispute; bad weather

    Not working but not seeking work for reasons other than in (c):

    (d) No work, futile to look[4]   _____weeks

    (e) Other reasons, such as student or
        housewife[5]   _____weeks

---

1. An alternative form for Questions 5 and 6 would involve asking separately about each period during the last twelve months when the person was not working and the major reason for not working during that period. Question 5 would then be: "What was the (first, second, . .) period when (he) (she) was not working?" The Continuous Longitudinal Manpower Survey (CLMS) conducted by the Census Bureau uses this approach. Such an approach might increase the probability of accurate responses.

2. If the answer given in response to this question indicates that the person was actually employed during the period but not attending work due to such reasons as sick leave or vacation, that incident should be considered as "employment." If all nonwork periods listed by respondent consist of time off from steady employment, the interviewer should change the answer to Question 4 from "yes" to "no."

3. Periods noted for this reason are times of unemployment under the usual definition which requires that an individual be seeking work.

4. Periods noted for this reason are times when an individual was a "discouraged worker."

5. This category provides a check on whether the respondent's indication of reason for not working is relevant to Measure 2 in Exhibit 1.

M-1   7. What was (name of adult household member) doing most of last week?

_____Employed

_____Employed but not at work ⎤——— GO TO Q8

_____Not employed   SKIP TO Q13

IF "EMPLOYED," ASK:

8. How many hours did (he) (she) work last week?

_____35 hours or more   SKIP TO Q12

_____Less than 35 hours   GO TO Q9

IF LESS THAN 35 HOURS, ASK:

9. Does (he) (she) usually work 35 hours or more hours per week at this job?

_____Yes   SKIP TO Q12

_____No   GO TO Q10

IF NO, ASK:

10. Would (he) (she) work more hours if (he) (she) had the opportunity?

_____Yes   GO TO Q11

_____No   SKIP TO Q12

IF YES, ASK:

11. What was the major reason (he) (she) did not work more hours?

_____No work available

_____Personal lack of skills/education

_____Lack of transportation

_____Family responsibilities/child care

M-4   12.   What is his/her (hourly wage) (or weekly earnings) (or monthly earnings) at this employment?

	TO BE CALCULATED LATER TO OBTAIN ANNUAL EQUIVALENT
Hourly $ _____	x 1,920 = $ _____
or	
Weekly $ _____	x 50 = $ _____
or	
Monthly $ _____	x 12 = $ _____

GO TO Q15

IF NOT EMPLOYED DURING PAST WEEK, ASK:

M-1
M-2   13.   Was (name of household member) looking for work last week?

_____Yes   SKIP TO Q15

_____No   GO TO Q14

M-1
M-2   14.   What was the major reason (name of household member) was not looking for work?

_____ Believes no work available in line of work or area

_____ Couldn't find any work

_____ Lacks necessary schooling/skills

_____ Employer thinks too young

_____ Can't arrange child care

_____ Family responsibilities

_____ In school or other training

_____ Ill health; disability

_____ Retired

_____ Other

ASK ONLY WITH REGARD TO RESPONDENT, IF RESPONDENT WAS "EMPLOYED" LAST WEEK; OTHERWISE GO TO Q16.

M-5 15. How would you rate the following characteristics of the job(s) you held last week?

	Excellent	Good	Fair	Poor
(a) Adequacy of earnings	___	___	___	___
(b) Opportunities for advancement	___	___	___	___
(c) Use of your skills	___	___	___	___
(d) Provision of healthy, pleasant, and safe working conditions	___	___	___	___
(e) Overall job rating	___	___	___	___

FOR EACH MEMBER OF THE HOUSEHOLD OVER 16 YEARS OLD, ASK:

M-7 16. In the past twelve months about how much did (name of household member) earn from wages and salaries before taxes and other deductions were taken out?

Member A $_____

Member B $_____

Member C $_____

TO BE CALCULATED LATER

TOTAL $_____

M-7 17. Did you or any other member of the household receive income from nonfarm self-employment, a professional practice, or partnership during the past twelve months?

_____Yes   GO TO Q18

_____No   SKIP TO Q19

IF YES, ASK FOR EACH SUCH HOUSEHOLD MEMBER:

M-7   18.   About how much did (he) (she) receive in net income?

Member A $_____ .

Member B $_____

Member C $_____

```
┌─────────────────────────────┐
│ TO BE CALCULATED LATER      │
│    TOTAL   $_____       │
└─────────────────────────────┘
```

M-7   19.   Did you or any other member of your household receive income from operation of (his) (her) own farm during the past twelve months?

_____Yes   GO TO Q20

_____No   SKIP TO Q21

IF YES, ASK FOR EACH SUCH HOUSEHOLD MEMBER:

M-7   20.   About how much did (he) (she) receive in net income from the farm?

Member A $_____

Member B $_____

Member C $_____

```
┌─────────────────────────────┐
│ TO BE CALCULATED LATER      │
│  ·TOTAL   $_____        │
└─────────────────────────────┘
```

M-7   21. During the past twelve months did you or any other member of your
            household receive any money from:

            (READ THE FOLLOWING LIST. IF "NO," WRITE "0." IF "YES," ASK
            "ABOUT HOW MUCH?" AND WRITE THE AMOUNT.)

            Estates, trusts, dividends, interest $_____

            Government or private pensions $_____

            Alimony or child support $_____

            Veterans payments (GI Bill) $_____

            Workman's compensation $_____

            Social Security or Railroad
            Retirement payments $_____

            Food stamps $_____ *

            Unemployment compensation or
            supplemental unemployment benefits $_____ *

            Aid to families with dependent
            children (AFDC) $_____ *

            Supplemental security income (SSI) $_____ *

            Other welfare or public assistance $_____ *

            Other income $_____

                    TO BE CALCULATED LATER

            (a) Total household income $_____
                (Q16 + Q18 + Q20 + Q21)

            (b) Transfer payments
                primarily intended to
                compensate low-income
                households (Q21 items
                with *) $_____

            (c) Household income before
                transfer payments to
                compensate low-income
                households (a minus b) $_____

M-11   22.   How would you rate your household's standard of living during the past twelve months?

    _____Excellent

    _____Good

    _____Fair

    _____Poor

    IF RESPONSE IS "POOR," ASK: Why do you say that? _____

M-11   23.   How would you rate your household's standard of living today as compared with one year ago?

    _____Much better

    _____Somewhat better

    _____Somewhat worse

    _____Much worse

    IF RESPONSE IS "MUCH WORSE," ASK: Why do you say that? _____

M-12   24.   How long have you lived here, in this house (apartment)?

    _____months

       or

    _____years

    IF ANSWER IS LESS THAN 12 MONTHS, ASK:

M-12   25.   From what state did you move to this address?

    _____ state

    IF ANSWER TO Q25 IS "THIS STATE," ASK:

M-12   26.   From what county did you move to this address?

    _____ county

ILLUSTRATIVE QUESTIONNAIRE FOR GATHERING
"QUALITY OF SERVICE" DATA FROM INDUSTRIAL CLIENTS [a]

INSTRUCTIONS:

It is preferable that the person who acted as liaison between your firm and (the state Industrial Development Office) complete this questionnaire. If you are this person, please fill in as much of the questionnaire as possible and return it. If this person is someone else, please route this to him/her. For your convenience, a postpaid return envelope is enclosed.

The questions are designed to obtain your initial, spontaneous response, so answer them quickly with the first response that comes to mind. If you are not sure of an answer, give an educated guess. Try not to leave any questions unanswered.

THANK YOU FOR YOUR ASSISTANCE.

---

1. Please estimate the extent to which your company used the service of the (state Industrial Development Office):

   _____ Very much
   _____ Somewhat
   _____ A little
   _____ Not at all

M-6

2. Listed below are characteristics associated with the services provided by the (state Industrial Development Office). The scales reflect the degree of positive or negative forms of each characteristic. Based on your company's experience, please mark the position on the scale as indicated in the following example:

   Slow ├──X───────────┤ Fast

The State Industrial Development Office

Not reliable	Reliable
Tardy	Prompt
Disorganized	Organized
Not relevant to firm's interests	Relevant to firm's interests
Not cooperative	Cooperative
Poorly informed	Well informed

Plant Site Tours by State Officials

_____ No site visit conducted

Biased	Unbiased
Disorganized	Organized
Not relevant to firm's interests	Relevant to firm's interests

---

[a] This questionnaire is illustrative and has not been tested. It can be used as the starting point in the development of an actual questionnaire which should be pretested with a small sample of firms prior to full use. One or more codes to the left of each question indicate the specific measure(s) in Exhibit 7 for which the question is to obtain data.

M-6   3. (a) What is your overall rating of the service you received from (state Industrial Development Office):

 _____ Excellent
 _____ Good
 _____ Fair
 _____ Poor

    (b) If fair or poor, why do you say that?

 _____

M-5   4. Please estimate the importance of the following factors as they pertain to your decision as to whether or not to locate in (name of state):[a]

	Very Positive Influence	Somewhat Positive Influence	Not an Influencing Factor Either Way	Somewhat Negative Influence	Very Negative Influence
Access to markets					
Amicable labor relations					
Lower wages in (name of the state)					
Availability of labor already in (name of state)					
Ease of attracting out-of-state skilled labor (including research personnel)					
Availability of raw materials					
Fuel cost					
Availability of capital					
Climate					
Community facilities (educational, utilities, police, and fire)					
Community attitudes and assistance					
State and/or municipal tax structure					
Assistance by:					
(a) State industrial development office					
(b) Local development groups					
(c) Banks, railroad, utilities					
(d) Private industrial consultants					
Personal considerations related to economic advantage (e.g., friendship with customers, suppliers, or bankers)					
Personal considerations unrelated to economic advantage (e.g., hometown of owner)					
Other (please specify)					

M-1(b)
M-3(b)
M-4(b)

_____

[a]Based on a similar question asked in a survey of Florida industrial prospects and discussed in Karaska and Bramhall, eds., Locational Analysis.

5. What is your position with the company?_____

6. Were you involved in the decision on the location or expansion of the plant in question?

                         _____Yes   _____No

7. If you answered yes to Question 6, what was the nature of your involvement?

     _____I had sole responsibility for making the decision.

     _____I participated with others in making a joint decision.

     _____I aided others who made the decision by securing information but did not participate in the decision itself.

     _____Other (please specify)_____

8. What was your firm's final decision?

     _____Locate in (state)

     _____Locate elsewhere

     _____Expand in (state)

     _____Expand elsewhere

     _____Not to locate or expand

     _____Decision not made

Appendix C
ILLUSTRATIVE QUESTIONNAIRE FOR A TOURISM
FOLLOW-UP SURVEY [a]

Introductory Letter
(for Mail Survey)

A few months ago you requested information on (name of state). By means of this questionnaire we hope to obtain your impressions of the information provided in response to that request and to see how you may have used it.

Your response will help improve the services (name of state) offers its visitors.

After answering the questions, place this questionnaire in the enclosed self-addressed, postage-stamped envelope and drop it in the mail.

Thank you,

(signature)

Telephone Introduction

Hello, my name is _____ from the (name of state) state government. A few months ago you requested information on (name of state). I'm calling now to ask you a few questions about your impressions of that material and to see how you may have used it in trip planning.

Questions

M-7 1. Did you receive information on (name of state) in the mail during the past six months?

_____Yes _____No _____Don't know

IF YOUR ANSWER TO QUESTION 1 IS "NO," SKIP TO QUESTION 4.

M-7 2. Please rate the information you received on the following characteristics:

	Excellent	Good	Fair	Poor
(a) Its completeness--the extent to which it contained the information you wanted.	____	____	____	____
(b) The speed with which you received it after requesting it.	____	____	____	____
(c) Its attractiveness.	____	____	____	____

---

[a]This list of questions is illustrative and has not been tested. Many of the questions are based on questions used in surveys in Texas, South Carolina, Pennsylvania, and Massachusetts. It can provide a starting point for developing a questionnaire which should be pretested. One or more codes to the left of each question indicate the specific measure(s) in Exhibit 9 for which the question is to obtain data.

3. What additional information or other improvements might make the information more helpful?_____

_____

M-5a
M-5b   4. Have you visited (name of state) in the past six month?

       _____Yes   _____No

       IF YOUR ANSWER TO QUESTION 4 IS "YES", GO TO QUESTION 5.
       IF YOUR ANSWER TO QUESTION 4 is "NO", GO TO QUESTION 8.

       <u>FOR THOSE WHO VISITED (NAME OF STATE) IN THE PAST SIX MONTHS</u>

5. Where did you go in (name of state)? Trace your approximate route on this map.

6. [IF CONDUCTED BY TELEPHONE, ASK:] What was your primary destination in (name of state)?

    (a) Did the information influence your decision to visit (name of state)

      _____Very Much [attracted your interest in visiting (name of state)]
      _____Somewhat [reinforced tentative plans to visit (name of state)]
      _____Not at all [already had firm plans to visit (name of state)]

    (b) Did the literature influence the length of your visit to (name of state)?

      _____Lengthened planned visit
      _____Shortened planned visit
      _____No effect on travel plans
      _____Trip plans not made when literature was received

M-5b   (c) Did the information influence your selection of places to visit in (name of state)

      _____Very much   _____Somewhat   _____Not at all

M-7   7. How useful was the information in planning your trip?

      _____Very useful   _____Somewhat useful   _____Not useful
    If it was "not useful," why?_____

THANK YOU.

FOR THOSE WHO HAVE NOT VISITED (NAME OF STATE) IN THE PAST SIX MONTHS

8. What was your main purpose at the time you requested literature on (name of state)?

   (a) _____No trip was contemplated; enjoy learning about other states

   (b) _____Was considering a trip which might include (name of state)

   (c) _____To help us plan a trip to or through (name of state)

9. Have you taken a vacation trip during the past six months?

   _____Yes   _____No

   IF "YES," ANSWER ONLY (a) AND (b)
   IF "NO," SKIP TO QUESTION 10

   (a) What state was the primary destination of that trip?

   _____

   (b) What factors led you to visit that state rather than (name of state)?

      _____Recreational opportunities
            What type?_____

      _____Relatives or friends there

      _____Distance to (name of state) too great

      _____Congestion or lack of accommodations in (name of state)

      _____Convention or business meeting

      _____Special or historical attractions

      _____Other (specify) _____

10. Are you planning a visit to (name of state)?

   _____Definitely   _____Possibly   _____Not presently

M-6

Appendix D
ILLUSTRATIVE QUESTIONNAIRE FOR GATHERING
OUTCOME DATA ON EMPLOYMENT AND TRAINING PROGRAMS[1]

Information Provided to Interviewer from Respondent's Records

1. Respondent's name.

2. Respondent's telephone number.

3. Name and phone number of friend or relative who would know of respondent's whereabouts (provided by respondent in program application) to be used if respondent cannot otherwise be reached.

4. Type of program in which respondent participated.

5. Location, name of employment or training project, or other identification of project in which respondent participated.

6. Dates of participation by respondent.

     *   *   *   *   *   *   *

1. What is your MAIN activity now?

    _____ Working
    _____ Attending school or a training program
    _____ Not working or attending school or a training program

M-1(a)
M-1(b)

2. What was the approximate data on which you (began this job) (began this school or training program) (last worked or attended a school or a training program)? (RECORD ANSWER ON ATTACHED TABULATION SHEET)

IF NOW WORKING: GO TO 3.
IF NOW ATTENDING SCHOOL OR A TRAINING PROGRAM: SKIP TO 11.
IF NOW NOT WORKING OR ATTENDING A SCHOOL OR TRAINING PROGRAM:
    SKIP TO 9.

---

    1. Several parts of this list of questions were adapted from continuous Longitudinal Manpower Survey (CLMS) and the Current Population Survey (CPS), both conducted by the Census Bureau. The set of questions presented here, however, has not been tested. The codes to the left of each question indicate the specific measure(s) in Exhibit 10 for which the question is to obtain data.

3. How many hours per week do you work in this job?

    _____ Hours

    IF 35 HOURS OR MORE: SKIP TO 5.
    IF LESS THAN 35 HOURS: GO TO 4.

4. Why did you work less than 35 hours last week?   (DO NOT READ LIST)

    _____ Cannot find full-time work
    _____ Full-time work is less than 35 hours
    _____ Do not want to work more hours
    _____ Other (SPECIFY)_____

M-2

5. What do you do in your present job?

    (JOB TITLE OR BRIEF DESCRIPTION)

    _____

    _____

    ┌───┐
    │ INTERVIEWER ESTIMATES WHETHER THIS JOB IS: │
    │ _____ Probably uses the training provided   │
    │ _____ Possibly uses the training provided   │
    │ _____ Probably doesn't use training   │
    │ _____ Unable to determine (REFER TO SUPERVISOR   │
    │   FOR DETERMINATION)   │
    └───┘

M-2
M-3

6. How often do you use the knowledge and skills which you acquired
    in the program in performing your present job?

    _____ Frequently
    _____ Sometimes
    _____ Seldom
    _____ Never

M-3

7. How do you feel about your present job?

    _____ Very satisfied
    _____ Somewhat satisfied
    _____ Somewhat dissatisfied
    _____ Very dissatisfied

    (IF "SOMEWHAT OR VERY DISSATISFIED," ASK: Why do you say that?)

    _____

    _____

M-3 8. How do you feel about opportunities for advancement in your present job?

_____ Excellent
_____ Good
_____ Fair
_____ Poor

SKIP TO 11

9. Are you looking for a job?

_____ Yes
_____ No

10. Why are you not presently looking for a job? (DO NOT READ LIST)

_____ No work available
_____ Lacks necessary schooling or training
_____ Employers think respondent is too young
_____ Can't arrange child care; family responsibilities
_____ Ill health; disability
_____ Other (SPECIFY) _____

M-1(a)
M-1(b) 11. What was your MAIN activity before (STATE STARTING DATE OF PREVIOUS ACTIVITY OR NAME OF PREVIOUS ACTIVITY)?

_____ Working
_____ Attending school or a training program
_____ Not working or attending a school or training program

M-1(a)
M-1(b) 12. When did you (begin that job) (begin that school or training course) (stop working or attending school or training prior to [date used in Q. 11])? _____

REPEAT QUESTIONS 11 AND 12 FOR EACH ACTIVITY PERIOD UNTIL THE POINT SIX (OR TWELVE) MONTHS PRIOR TO PROGRAM ENTRY IS REACHED. THE RESPONSES SHOULD BE ENTERED ON THE "WORK HISTORY" FORM ATTACHED.

M-5(a)
M-5(b)

13. Are you or your family NOW:

(STATE EACH ITEM ON THE FOLLOWING LIST SEPARATELY,
REPEATING QUESTION 12 IF NECESSARY)

Yes   No   Don't Know

___   ___   ___   Living in public housing or paying a lower rent because the government is paying part of the cost?

___   ___   ___   Buying or receiving food stamps?

___   ___   ___   Receiving any welfare payments from AFDC or supplemental security income (yellow or gold checks)?

___   ___   ___   Receiving any other payments from public assistance or welfare?

___   ___   ___   Are YOU now receiving unemployment compensation?

M-4(a)
M-4(b)

14. During the last six (or twelve) months since leaving the program have you earned any money from employment?

_____ Yes
_____ No

(IF YES): How much did you earn before taxes and other deductions were taken out? $_____

M-5(b) 15. In the six (or twelve) months BEFORE you entered the program, that is, from (date six [or twelve] months before entry) to (date of entry), did you or your family:

(STATE EACH ITEM IN THE FOLLOWING LIST SEPARATELY, REPEATING QUESTION 14 IF NECESSARY)

Yes	No	Don't Know	
___	___	___	Live in public housing or pay a lower rent because the government was paying part of the cost?
___	___	___	Buy or receive food stamps?
___	___	___	Receive any welfare payments from AFDC or supplemental security income (yellow or gold checks)?
___	___	___	Receive any other payments from public assistance?
___	___	___	Were YOU receiving any unemployment compensation?

M-4(b) 16. In the six (or twelve) months BEFORE you entered the program did you earn any money from employment?

_____ Yes
_____ No

(IF YES): How much did you earn before taxes and other deductions were taken out? $_____

M-7 17. How would you rate the extent to which the program helped you to obtain employment?

_____ Very helpful
_____ Somewhat helpful
_____ Of only minor help
_____ Not helpful

M-7 18. How would you rate the extent to which the program helped you perform and keep the job?

_____ Very helpful
_____ Somewhat helpful
_____ Of only minor help
_____ Not helpful

TABULATION OF RESPONDENT'S WORK HISTORY[1]

INSTRUCTIONS: (a) Mark the response to Question 2 by drawing a vertical line downward in the proper column in the chart below (determined by Question 1) to the month when the activity was begun.

(b) Ask Questions 3 and 4 regarding present job.

(c) Complete the week history by repeating Questions 11 and 12 for each activity prior to respondent's present activity, beginning with the immediately prior activity and working backwards. Mark the work history chart by drawing a vertical line downward from the date indicated by Question 11 to the date indicated by Question 12 until reaching the month six or twelve months prior to program entry.

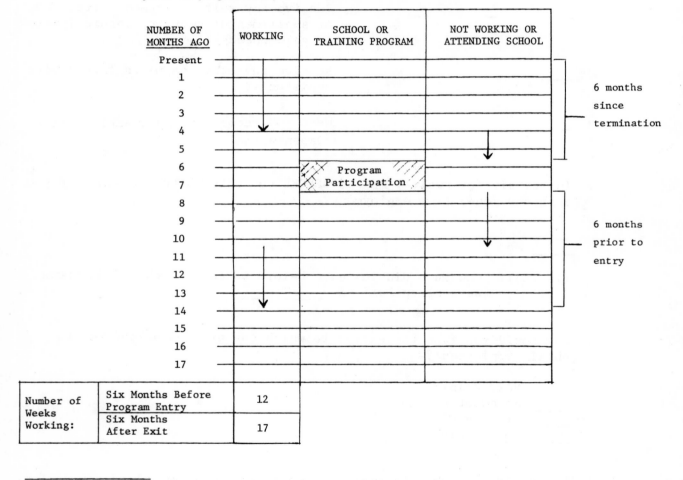

Number of Weeks Working:	Six Months Before Program Entry	12
	Six Months After Exit	17

---

1. For illustrative purposes, this portion of the questionnaire has been filled out, reflecting the following work history: (a) respondent is now employed and has been employed for seventeen weeks; (b) respondent was in a training program for six weeks, was unemployed upon exit for seven weeks; and (c) respondent was employed until thirteen weeks prior to program entry.

SELECTED BIBLIOGRAPHY

SELECTED BIBLIOGRAPHY

Overall Economic Development

Andrews, Richard Bruce. Wisconsin's Planning Methods and Potentials. Land Economics Monograph no. 2. Madison: University of Wisconsin Press, 1968.

California, State Department of Finance, Audits Division. Development, Implementation, and Evaluation of Program Effectiveness Measurement in California State Government, with Emphasis on Air Quality Programs. Sacramento, December 1974.

DaVanzo, Julie. An Analytical Framework for Studying the Potential Effects of an Income Maintenance Program on U.S. Interregional Migration (R-1081.-EDA). Santa Monica, Calif.: The Rand Corporation, December 1972.

Mushkin, Selma J. State Programming and Economic Development. Chicago: Council of State Governments and George Washington University, June 1965.

North Carolina, Department of Natural and Economic Resources and Department of Administration, Office of State Planning (Interagency Task Force). North Carolina Environmental Indicators. Raleigh, 1973.

North Carolina, Division of State Budget and Management, Department of Administration. Guide to the Use of Economic Effectiveness Measurements. Raleigh, May 1977.

_____. How the Survey Was Conducted and What It Cost. Raleigh, May 1977.

_____. How the Survey Was Conducted and What It Cost. Raleigh, May 1977.

_____. How Well Off Are North Carolinians? Raleigh, May 1977.

Phelps, Edmund S. The Goal of Economic Growth. New York: W. W. Norton and Co., 1962.

Revzan, Lawrence H. An Evaluation of Policy-Related Research in the Field of Municipal Economic Development. 3 vols. Washington, D.C.: Ernst and Ernst, September 1974.

Rulison, Michael V. E., and Branch, Constance L. Indicators of Social and Economic Well-Being in North Carolina. Research Memorandum RM-ON-641-1. Research Triangle Park, N.C.: Research Triangle Institute, Operations Research and Economics Division, August 1971.

Stigler, George J. The Goals of Economic Policy. From the Henry Simmons
    Lectures, University of Chicago Law School. Chicago: University of
    Chicago Press, 1958.

Sum, Andrew M. "Labor Market Information from a User's Perspective: Data
    Inputs for CETA Planning Purposes." Presentation to Labor Market
    Information Seminar, 17 December 1975, in Atlanta, Ga.

_____. "Labor Market Information Inputs for Local Manpower Planning and
    Evaluation." N.p., April 1976.

U.S., Congress, Congressional Budget Office. Poverty Status of Families
    Under Alternative Definitions of Income. Background Paper no. 17,
    13 January 1977.

U.S., Department of Commerce, Bureau of the Census. Consumer Income.
    Current Population Reports, Series P-60, no. 79. Washington, D.C.:
    Government Printing Office, 27 July 1971.

_____. Mobility of the Population of the United States: March 1970 to
    March 1974. Current Population Reports, Series P-20, no. 273.
    Washington, D.C.: Government Printing Office, 1974.

_____. Money Income in 1973 of Families and Persons in the United States.
    Current Population Reports, Series P-60, no. 97. Washington, D.C.:
    Government Printing Office, 1975.

_____. The Current Population Survey: An Overview. Washington, D.C.:
    Government Printing Office, January 1975. Reprinted from Annals of
    Economic and Social Measurement, vol. 2, no. 2 (April 1973).

_____. The Current Population Survey: A Report on Methodology. Technical
    Paper no. 7. Washington, D.C.: Government Printing Office, 1963.

_____. Data Access Descriptions, DAD No. 37, Micro-data from the Current
    Population Survey: The Annual Demographic File. Washington, D.C.:
    Government Printing Office, December 1974.

U.S., Department of Labor, Bureau of Labor Statistics. BLS Handbook of
    Methods. Bulletin 1910. Washington, D.C., 1976.

Van Alstyne, Carol. The State We're In: A Candid Appraisal of Manpower and
    Economic Development. Durham, N.C.: The North Carolina Fund, 1 June 1967.

Wertheimer, Richard F., II. The Monetary Rewards of Migration Within the
    U.S. Washington, D.C.: The Urban Institute, March 1970.

Wright, Ward and Benson, Virginia B. "Your Local Economy: Does City Hall
    Play a Role?" Nation's Cities (National League of Cities) 1, no. 9
    (September 1972).

Industrial Development

Chicago, Mayor's Committee for Economic and Cultural Development, Mid-Chicago Economic Development Project. A Partnership for Action: The Mid-Chicago Economic Development Project. Chicago, May 1970.

Hart, Christine H. "How Should Our City Grow?--Governing Industrial Growth in Liberty, Mo." In Management Information Service. Washington, D.C.: International City Management Association, January 1977.

Hunker, Henry L. Industrial Development. Lexington, Mass.: Lexington Books, D.C. Heath and Co., 1974.

Ohio, Department of Economic and Community Development, Economic Development Division. Appalachian Selective Development Program Final Report. Columbus, Ohio, 9 February 1973.

Pennsylvania, Office of Administration, Budget Bureau, Division of Program Audit. A Program Audit Report on the Industrial Development Program in Pennsylvania. Harrisburg, Pa., April 1971.

Perloff, Harvey S.; Dunn, Edgar S.; Lampard, Eric E.; and Muth, Richard G. Regions, Resources, and Economic Growth. Baltimore: Johns Hopkins Press, 1960.

Sample, James C. Patterns of Regional Economic Change: A Quantitative Analysis of U.S. Regional Growth and Development. Cambridge, Mass.: Ballinger Publishing Company, 1974.

U.S., Advisory Commission on Intergovernmental Relations. Urban and Rural America: Policies for Future Growth. Washington, D.C.: Government Printing Office, April 1968.

U.S., Congress, House, Committee on Public Works. The Economic Adjustment Act of 1974 and Extending and Amending the Public Works and Economic Development Act of 1965: Hearings before the Subcommittee on Economic Development on H.R. 12942 and Related Bills. 93d Cong., 2d sess., 1974.

U.S., Department of Commerce. A Comparative Analysis of the Impacts Resulting from 50 Public Works Projects, 1970, 1974. Washington, D.C., December 1974.

U.S., Department of Commerce, Bureau of the Census, Social and Economic Statistics Administration, Publication Services Division. Mini-Guide to the 1972 Economic Censuses, by Valerie M. McFarland and Elizabeth M. Jackson. Washington, D.C., 1972.

U.S., Department of Commerce, Economic Development Administration. EDA in Oakland: A 1974 Update, by William J. Tobin. Washington, D.C. 1974.

_____. Evaluation of EDA's Urban Program. Vol. I: Pilot Test in Chicago, Illinois and vol. II: Methodology. Washington, D.C.: Government Printing Office, April 1971.

_____. Evaluation of Seven Major Technical Assistance Projects with National Scope. Washington, D.C.: Government Printing Office, October 1971.

_____. Summary of Case Studies: Evaluation of EDA Rural Development Activities in Fifteen Areas. Washington, D.C.: Program Analysis Division, Economic Development Administration, Spring 1970.

Tourism Promotion

Arthur D. Little, Inc. Tourism and Recreation: A State of the Art Study. Washington, D.C.: U.S. Department of Commerce, Economic Development Administration, 1967.

Bearden James H. The Travel Industry in North Carolina. Greenville, N.C.: East Carolina College, 1964.

Bird, Ronald, and Miller, Frank. Contributions of Tourist Trade to Incomes of People in Missouri Ozarks. Columbia, Mo.: University of Missouri, 1962.

Chicago, Illinois. Market Research Program, 1967 - 1971. Chicago: Chicago Convention and Tourism Bureau, Tourism Division, 1972.

Cook, Suzanne D. A Survey of Definitions in U.S. Domestic Tours of Studies. Washington, D.C.: U.S. Travel Data Center, 25 June 1975.

Cramer-Krasselt Company. Analysis of Advertising Inquiries. Prepared for Wisconsin Conservation Department. Madison, Wis.: Cramer-Krasselt Co., n.d.

Florida Tourist Study: 1961-1966. Tallahassee, Fla.: State of Florida, n.d.

Frechtling, Douglas C. "A Model State Continuing Travel Research Program." Paper presented to Discover America Travel Institute, Educational Seminar for State Travel Officials, 30 June 1975, at Ohio State University.

Friedman, Robert S. How States Find Out About Their Tourist Trade. College Park, Md.: University of Maryland, 1954.

Goeldner, C. R., and Dicke, Karen. *Bibliography of Tourism and Travel: Research Studies, Reports and Articles*. 3 vols.: *National Studies, State Studies, Foreign Studies*. Boulder, Colo.: University of Colorado, 1971.

Keeling, William B. *The Georgia Travel Industry 1960-1970*. Athens, Ga.: University of Georgia, 1971.

Ketchum, MacLeod, and Grove, Inc. *Survey Among Persons Requesting Travel Information from the Commonwealth of Pennsylvania*. N.p., January 1971.

McIntosh, Robert W. *Tourism Principals, Practices, and Philosophies*. Columbus, Ohio: Grid, Inc., 1972.

Montana, State Highway Commission. *Five Years of Tourist Studies in Montana*. Helena, Mont.: October 1963.

Nolan, Sidney D. *Response Evaluation of Selected Texas Tourism Advertising*. Austin: Tourist Development Agency and Agricultural Experiment Station, State of Texas, August 1973.

North Carolina. *1974 North Carolina Travel Survey*. Raleigh: Department of Natural and Economic Resources, 1975.

North Dakota, State Highway Department, Planning and Research Division. *North Dakota Survey of Out of State Visitors: Technical Report*. Bismarck, March 1972.

O'Donnell, Edward T. *An Essay on Methods of Measurement of Employment Directly Generated by Tourism in Massachusetts in 1958 - 1967*. Boston: State of Massachusetts, 1969.

Oklahoma, Department of Highways, and The University of Oklahoma Bureau of Business Research. *Out of State Passenger Travel in Oklahoma 1962 - 1963*. Oklahoma City, 1964.

Pennington, Allan L.; Ross, Ivan; and Rudelius, William. *Minnesota Tourism, 1968: A Market Analysis*. St. Paul, Minn.: Minnesota State Planning Agency, 1969.

Research Triangle Institute. *The 1973 North Carolina Travel Survey*. Raleigh: Department of Natural and Economic Resources, State of North Carolina, 1974.

Rovelstad, James M. *Analytical Measures of Travel and Tourism for States and Smaller Areas: The West Virginia Model*. West Virginia University Business and Economic Studies, vol. 12, no. 2. Morgantown, W.Va.: West Virginia University, Bureau of Business Research, July 1974.

U.S. Travel Data Center. *Survey of State Travel Offices: 1974-75*. Washington, D.C.: U.S. Travel Data Center, 1974.

U.S., Department of Commerce, Bureau of the Census. Census of Transportation, National Travel Survey, 1972. Washington, D.C.: Government Printing Office, 1973.

Woodside, Arch G. "Advertising Campaign Conversions Study, 1972." Columbia: Department of Parks, Recreation, and Tourism, State of South Carolina, Summer 1973.

Employment and Training

Ashenfelter, Orley. "Manpower Training and Earnings." Monthly Labor Review, April 1975.

Backer, Thomas E. Methods of Assessing the Disadvantages in Manpower Programs: A Review and Analysis. Research and Development Findings no. 14. Washington, D.C.: Human Interaction Research Institute, 1973.

Bateman, Worth. "An Application of Cost-Benefit Analysis to the Work Experience Program." American Economic Review 57, no. 2 (May 1967).

Borus, Michael E., ed. Evaluating the Impact of Manpower Programs. Lexington, Mass.: Lexington Books, 1972.

_____, and Tash, William R. Measuring the Impact of Manpower Programs: A Primer. Policy Papers in Human Resources and Industrial Relations no. 17. Ann Arbor, Mich.: Institute of Labor and Industrial Relations, November 1970.

District of Columbia. Manpower Planning: The State of the Art. Washington, D.C.: D.C. Government, April 1973.

Dorsey, John Wesley, Jr. "The Mack Case: A Study in Unemployment." Ph.D. dissertation. Cambridge: Harvard University, June 1963.

Fechter, Alan. Forecasting the Impact of Technological Change on Manpower Utilization and Displacement: An Analytic Summary. Washington, D.C.: The Urban Institute, March 1975.

Fulmer, John L., and Robinson, James W. "Worker Mobility and Government Aid." Business and Government Review (School of Business and Public Administration, University of Missouri), September-October 1968.

Hawaii, Department of Labor and Industrial Relations, Research and Statistics Office. Estimation of Employment and Unemployment in Hawaii. Honolulu: February, 1974.

Lampman, Robert J. "Population Change and Poverty Reduction, 1947-1975." In Leo Fishman, ed., Poverty and Affluence. New Haven: Yale University Press, 1966. Reprint 2, Institute for Research on Poverty. Madison: University of Wisconsin, 1966.

Levine, Robert A. "Systems Analysis in the War on Poverty." Presented at 29th National Meeting of Operations Research Society of America, 18-20 May 1966, Santa Monica, Calif.

Morton, J. E. Handbook for Community Manpower Surveys. Methods for Manpower Analysis, no. 5. Washington, D.C.: The W. E. Upjohn Institute for Employment Research, October 1972.

Nay, Joe N.; Scanlon, John W.; and Wholey, Joseph S. Benefits and Costs of Manpower Training Programs: A Synthesis of Previous Studies with Reservations and Recommendations. Washington, D.C.: The Urban Institute, March 1973.

New York State, Legislative Commission on Expenditure Review. Summary: Manpower Training in New York State. Albany, N.Y., February 1971.

Page, David A. Retraining Under the Manpower Development Act: A Cost-Benefit Analysis. Washington, D.C.: The Brookings Institution, December 1964.

Pub. L. No. 93-203. (1973).

Scanlon, John W.; Buchanan, Garth; Nay, Joe; and Wholey, Joseph. An Evaluation System to Support Planning, Allocation and Control in a Decentralized, Comprehensive Manpower Program. WAshington, D.C.: The Urban Insitute, March 1971.

Sewell, David. Training the Poor: Rationale for a Benefit-Cost Evaluation of MITCE. Durham, N.C.: Committee on Manpower and Economic Development, March 1967.

Siebert, Glenn A. Effectiveness Indicators for Employment Offices: A Systems Approach. Working Paper no. 221, Institute of Urban and Regional Development. Berkeley, Calif.: University of California, September 1973.

Stromsdorfer, Ernest W. Cost-Effectiveness Studies of Vocational and Technical Education: A Comprehensive Bibliography. Council of Planning Librarians Exchange Bibliography no. 362. Bloomington, Ind.: Indiana University, January 1973.

U.S., Department of Commerce, Bureau of the Census, Social and Economic Statistics Administration. "LMS-8 Interviewer's Reference Manual, Longitudinal Manpower Survey." Washington, D.C.: Government Printing Office, n.d.

U.S., Department of Commerce, Bureau of the Census, and Department of Labor, Bureau of Statistics. Concepts and Methods Used in Manpower Statistics from the Current Population Survey. BLS Report no. 313. Current Population Reports, Series P-23, no. 22. Washington, D.C.: Government Printing Office, June 1967.

U.S., Department of Labor. <u>A Sharper Look at Unemployment in U.S. Cities</u>
<u>and Slums</u>. Washington, D.C.: Government Printing Office, March-April
1967.

U.S., Department of Labor, Bureau of Statistics. <u>Tomorrow's Manpower Needs,</u>
<u>National Manpower Projections and a Guide to their Use as a Tool in</u>
<u>Developing State and Area Manpower Projections</u>. Washington, D.C.:
Government Printing Office, February 1969.

U.S., Department of Labor, Manpower Administration. <u>ESARS Handbook</u>. Chap. 7,
"Report Preparation." Washington, D.C.: July 1974.

_____. <u>Job Analysis for Human Resource Management: A Review of Selected</u>
<u>Research and Development</u>, by Michael Wilson. Manpower Research Mono-
graph no. 36. Washington, D.C.: Government Printing Office, 1974.

_____. <u>POSARS Handbook</u>. Rev. ed. Washington, D.C., December 1974.

U.S., Office of Economic Opportunity. <u>A Framework for the Evaluation of</u>
<u>Training Programs</u> (staff paper), by Henry S. Terrell. Washington, D.C.:
20 September 1966.